ROUTE 66

TRAVEL THROUGH THE BIBLE

PositiveAction
BIBLE CURRICULUM

ROUTE 66: TRAVEL THROUGH THE BIBLE

Written by Mark Reed

Third Edition 2007
Sixth Printing 2019

Printed in the United States of America

ISBN 978-1-59557-109-0

Edited by Steve Braswell and C.J. Harris
Design by Shannon Brown
Chapter Artwork by Del Thompson

Published by

PositiveAction
FOR CHRIST

CONTENTS

UNIT ONE:
HOW IT ALL BEGAN

WHERE DID THE BIBLE COME FROM?

WHAT A BOOK!

The word *Bible* means _____. The Bible is the most important book ever written. It has been translated into more languages, published by more companies in more versions and editions, and sold more copies than any other book in the world.

The Bible is also called _____, which means _____. Because this book contains the words that _____ spoke and commanded men to write down, it is called _____.

According to 2 Timothy 3:16–17, all Scripture is _____, which means "_____." That is, the words in the Bible are from God. What was written down was precisely what God wanted to say.

According to 2 Peter 1:16–21, God inspired men through the _____. He spoke to them. Then they wrote His words to other people. Using a Bible dictionary, write the definition of *inspiration* in the following box:

Define *inspiration*:

God used many people to write the Bible—likely several dozen different individuals. Many of them are unknown. For example, no one knows for sure who wrote the books of _____ or _____, which were written around _____ B.C. and A.D. _____, respectively. Some books like Joshua and the prophets would appear to be named after the authors, but we have no specific biblical evidence. Still, the Bible is one unit. All of the books fit together to tell one story. This harmony of writings by different authors who lived many years apart shows that one mind guided them.

Read Exodus 34:27 and 1 Corinthians 2:10–13 to learn how God guided the human authors of the Bible.

- _____

- _____

God told some writers exactly what to write down. Moses, for example, wrote down the laws as God dictated them (Exo. 34:27–28). Other writers wrote about what they saw and heard. For example, Matthew, a disciple of Jesus, wrote about the things he saw Jesus do and what he heard Him say. Some writers, such as Luke, investigated and wrote down what others told them (Luke 1:1–4). Some authors copied the history from other books (2 Sam. 1:17–27). The Holy Spirit guided all of these men and their methods so that whatever they wrote was true.

People communicate in two basic ways.

- _____

- _____

God has spoken to humankind in these two ways.

As you read John 1:1, 14; 14:9–11, and Hebrews 1:1–2, discover how God has spoken to us in these ways. Then fill in the following:

- God's _____ are summarized in the _____.
- God's _____ are summarized in _____.

HOW IT ALL ADDS UP

As you read the following information, fill in the appropriate Bible division charts. Use the contents page in your Bible to fill in the name of each book.

- Law—Moses wrote these first five books of the Bible. They describe the beginning of time, the beginning of the world, and the beginning of God's nation, Israel.

- History—The books Joshua through Esther cover 1,000 years of Israel's history, recording Israel's conquest of the land that God promised and how the nation rose and fell under its judges, kings, and prophets.

- Poetry—This section is also called Wisdom Literature because wise men wrote their advice in these books. They include poems, songs, story-poems and wise sayings, and teachings. Except for Job, each of these books was written in the days of David and Solomon.

- Major prophets—Because these books are longer than the other prophets' writings, they are called major. The four authors, all prophets, lived during the time of Israel's kings. Lamentations is also a book of poetry.

Define *prophet*:

Define *prophecy*:

- Minor prophets—These twelve prophets who wrote shorter books also lived during the time of Israel's kings.

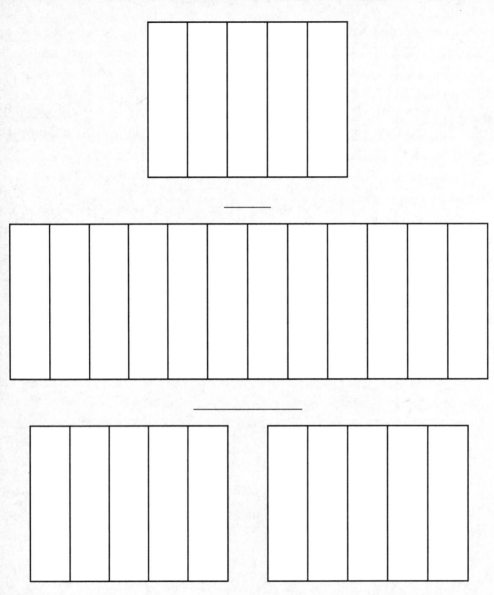

LESSON 2
GENESIS

IN THE BEGINNING...

GENESIS MEANS "BEGINNING"

Genesis is a book of beginnings.

- The beginning of _____ (1:1–25)

- The beginning of _____ and _____ (1:26–2:25)

- The beginning of _____ in the _____ (3:1–7)

- The beginning of _____ and _____ (3:8–24)

- The beginning of _____ _____ (4:1–4)

- The beginning of _____, _____ and _____ (4:17–22)

- The beginning of _____ (10:1–32; 11:1–9)

- The beginning of the _____ _____ (12:2)

God prepared _____ to write Genesis by having him trained to read and write in the palace of _____ of _____ (Exo. 2:1–10). God spoke to him at _____ _____ (Exo. 3:1), which is another name for Mount Sinai. God also commanded him to write down the laws that are recorded in Exodus through Deuteronomy.

In the first verse of Genesis, God tells us the most important facts we must know about Him. Write those facts in the blanks.

When: _____

Who: _____

G E N E S I S

ABRAHAM

THE CITY OF UR

Abram, whose name God later changed to Abraham, grew up in a city called Ur of the Chaldees. The Chaldees lived in the area of what is today Iraq and built magnificent cities. In Ur's famous schools and libraries, students learned reading and writing. They wrote with sticks on clay tablets. Many of these tablets, or "books," have been found at Ur and other ruined cities where the Chaldeans lived.

Citizens of Ur worshipped the moon-god, Nannar. Sometimes they offered human sacrifices to her. Using the following verses, trace on the map Abraham's journey from Ur to Canaan: Genesis 11:31; 12:1, 4–5.

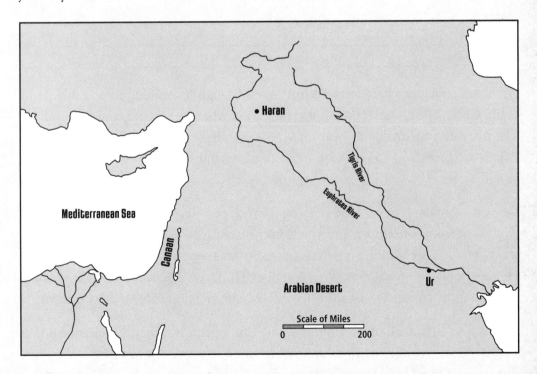

GOD PROMISED ABRAHAM...

Match the following verses to the appropriate promises. Write the letter of the references in the blanks to the left of the promise.

	1.	His children would become a great nation.	12:2a
	2.	God would bless those who blessed him.	12:2b
	3.	His descendants would own the land of Canaan.	12:3a
	4.	He and Sarah would have a son.	12:3b
	5.	All nations would be blessed by one of his descendants.	12:3c; 22:18
	6.	God would protect Abraham like a shield.	12:7
	7.	He would be a great man who would bless others.	15:1
	8.	God would curse his enemies.	18:1–15

...AND ABRAHAM BELIEVED GOD

Write Genesis 15:6 in the following space: _____
_____
_____

Abraham believed what God told him, even though it sounded impossible. How could God make his descendants a great nation when he was old, had no children, and his wife was unable to bear children? Abraham asked questions (15:2) and wondered how God would keep His promises, but he never doubted that God would do it.

Do you ever wonder how God is going to work out His promises? Maybe He asks you to control your temper, and you think you can't. Maybe He asks you to tell the truth, but you are afraid. Sometimes it seems as though God doesn't mean what He says in His promises. But when you obey Him, you discover that with His help you *can* do whatever He asks (Phil. 4:13). It's never as impossible as you think!

Just like Abraham, all of us wonder about God's plan. But that doesn't mean that we lose faith. We still believe that God is going to carry out His plan. We're just not sure about all of the details of that plan.

God rewards faith. Abraham believed, and God counted that faith as righteousness. God declared him to be righteous, in spite of his faults, because he believed. Do you think that God does the same with us?

Define *faith*:

Read Romans. 3:22–24. According to Paul, how does a person become good (righteous and just)? _____

_____

The implication is that when God sees believers, He sees neither their sinfulness nor some goodness that they have produced, but rather the righteousness of His holy Son.

One of the greatest demonstrations of Abraham's faith is found in Genesis 22:1–18. After reading that passage, check T (true) or F (false) for each statement.

- ☐ T | ☐ F 1. God told Abraham to go to the mountain to sacrifice his only son, Isaac.
- ☐ T | ☐ F 2. God demanded a sacrifice because He was angry with Abraham.
- ☐ T | ☐ F 3. Abraham refused to go.
- ☐ T | ☐ F 4. Isaac did not know that he was to be the sacrifice.
- ☐ T | ☐ F 5. God provided a ram to take Isaac's place on the altar.
- ☐ T | ☐ F 6. Abraham named the place *Yahweh-jireh*, or "The Lord will provide."

THINK ABOUT IT

What was God revealing about Himself when He called Abram out of a land of idolatry to become the father of a great nation with a special relationship to God?

_____

_____

_____

L E S S O N 5
G E N E S I S
WHO'S WHO?

ISRAEL'S FAMILY TREE

Abraham's family multiplied just as God had promised. Place the following names on Israel's family tree on the following page. Wives' names go in the box that is connected by a broken line to their husbands' names. Be sure to match the twelve sons of Jacob with the right mothers. Names go in order of birth, starting with the eldest at the top.

Abraham	Dan (30:4–6)	Sarah
Isaac	Naphtali (30:7–8)	Rebekah (24:61–67)
Jacob (25:21–26)	Gad (30:9–11)	Leah (29:32)
Esau (25:21–26)	Asher (30:12–13)	Rachel (30:22–23)
Reuben (29:32)	Issachar (30:17–18)	Bilhah (30:1–5)
Simeon (29:33)	Zebulun (30:19–20)	Zilpah (30:9)
Levi (29:34)	Joseph (30:22–24)	Edomites (36:8–9)
Judah (29:35)	Benjamin (35:16–18)	

WHAT HAPPENED NEXT?

- God changed _Jacob_ name to _Israel_ (35:9–10).
- _Joseph's brother_ threw him into a _pit_ because they were jealous of him because Jacob had given him a _coat of many colors_ and he had told them about his dreams of _ruling_ over his family (37:1–24).

27

ISRAEL'S FAMILY TREE

Abraham	Sarah
Isaac	Rebekah (24:61–67)
Jacob (25:21–26)	Leah (29:32)
Esau (25:21–26)	Rachel (30:22–23)
Reuben (29:32)	Bilhah (30:1–5)
Simeon (29:33)	Zilpah (30:9)
Levi (29:34)	Edomites (36:8–9)
Judah (29:35)	Dan (30:4–6)
	Naphtali (30:7–8)
	Gad (30:9–11)
	Asher (30:12–13)
	Issachar (30:17–18)
	Zebulun (30:19–20)
	Joseph (30:22–24)
	Benjamin (35:16–18)

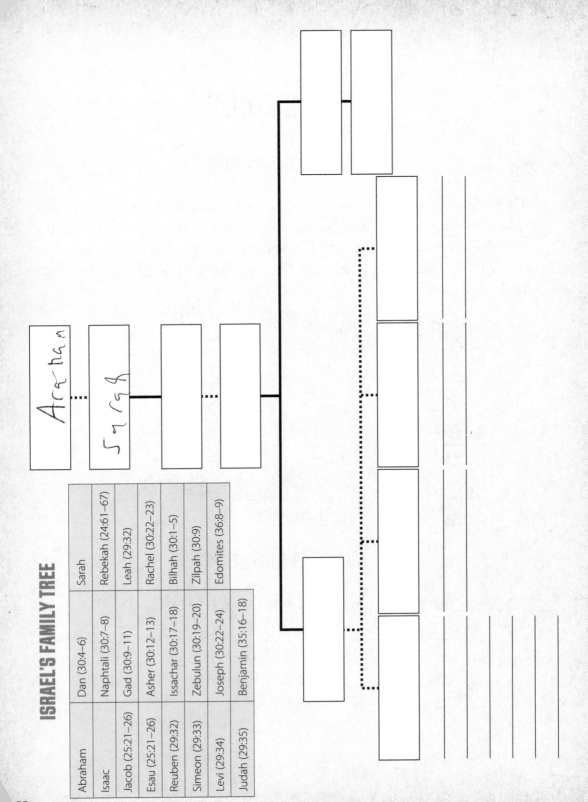

Abraham

Sarah

- The _Ishmaelites_ bought _Joseph_ as a slave and took him to Egypt where they sold him to _Potiphar_, the captain of Pharaoh's guard (37:25–36).

- Joseph went to prison because _Potiphar's wife_ falsely accused him. Nonetheless, Joseph succeeded in whatever he did because _the Lord was with_ (39:1–23).

- Joseph got out of prison by _interpreting dreams_

- Pharaoh put Joseph in charge of _the land of Egypt_

- Joseph stored up _food_ for _7_ years. He saved Egypt from a _famine_ that lasted _7_ years (41:1–57).

- Joseph's brothers bowed before him to ask for _food_ (42:1–26).

Extra Assignment: (The answers to the following questions are found somewhere in the chapters in Genesis that we have covered in this lesson.)

- Jacob's wife Leah also had a daughter named _Dinah_.

- Joseph's two sons were named _Manasseh_ and _Ephraim_

THINK ABOUT IT

What does Genesis 50:20 reveal about God's purposes for Joseph's slavery and imprisonment? _It reveals that God planned this 20 years before_

UNIT TWO:
DELIVERANCE

E X O D U S

GETTING OUT OF EGYPT

DOWN AND OUT IN EGYPT

The book of Exodus picks up the story of Abraham's descendants about 300 years after the end of Genesis. Exodus 1:6–14 summarizes what happened during those years. After reading it, see if you can fill in the following blanks:

After _Joseph_'s death, the children of Israel were made _slave_ by the _Pharuoh_. Still they grew in _number_ and became a great nation. The _Egyptian_ feared the Israelites because _they were so many of them_. This fulfilled God's prophecy to Abraham that his descendants would be enslaved and mistreated for _400_ years in a foreign land (see Gen. 15:13).

When Israel (Jacob) took his family to Egypt at the end of Genesis, there were _70_ family members altogether (Gen. 46:27). By the time they left Egypt, there were about _600,000_ fighting men, besides women and children (Exo. 12:37), meaning that the total number of people was probably at least _2m_.

The book of Exodus gets its name from the main event in the book, which is _the Exit out of Egypt_.

This fulfilled God's promise to Abraham in Genesis 15:14 that _God bring them out of Egypt via his great power_. God heard the Israelites' _groaning & cry_ and decided that the time had come to _fulfill his promise_ (Exo. 2:23–25).

Genesis is a book of ___*family*___ history, while Exodus is a book of
___*National*___ history. In Exodus, the nation of ___*Israel*___ travels from
___*Egypt*___ to ___*Mt Sinai*___. Locate these places on a map.

GOD'S MAN FOR THE MOMENT

Read Exodus 1–4 and select the best answers to complete the following statements:

B	1. Pharaoh was
	A. the name of an Egyptian. B. the title of the king of Egypt. C. the king's right-hand man.
C	2. The main character of Exodus who became the greatest leader of Israel was
	A. Joshua. B. Levi. C. Moses.
A	3. Pharaoh ordered Hebrew parents to throw their male babies into the river because
	A. the Hebrew people had become too many and too strong. B. there wasn't enough food to go around. C. he hated the Hebrews.
B	4. Who found a baby in a basket floating on the river?
	A. Pharaoh's servants B. Pharaoh's daughter C. The Hebrew midwives
C	5. Moses fled Egypt because
	A. two Hebrews learned that he had killed an Egyptian. B. Pharaoh learned that he was a Hebrew and wanted to kill him. C. Pharaoh wanted to kill him because he killed an Egyptian.
C	6. Moses married_____, the daughter of_____.
	A. Miriam, Midian B. Miriam, Pharaoh C. Zipporah, Jethro

B	7. Mt. Horeb is also called Mt. Sinai and

A. the mountain of fire.
B. the mountain of God.
C. Israel's mountain.

C	8. God called to Moses on Mt. Horeb from a

A. dark cloud that thundered.
B. pillar of fire that burned everything.
C. bush that burned but wasn't consumed.

A	9. God told Moses to

A. ask Pharaoh to release the Israelites.
B. lead Israel in battle against the Egyptians.
C. lead Israel out of Egypt secretly.

B	10. When Moses asked God's name, God said,

A. "The Lord God."
B. "I Am."
C. "The God of Abraham."

B	11. God promised Moses to bring Israel out of slavery in Egypt and into

A. Jericho.
B. a land of milk and honey.
C. the Red Sea.

A	12. God gave Moses _____ miracles to convince Pharaoh that he was God's prophet.

A. three
B. seven
C. ten

B	13. Who went with Moses to Pharaoh?

A. His wife
B. His brother, Aaron
C. The elders of Israel

TEN NASTY PLAGUES

Pharaoh scoffed at Moses' demand. He scoffed at the words of Israel's God. His nation depended on Hebrew slave labor. To let them go would be like giving away half of his wealth. So God proved His power and authority to Pharaoh by plagues. God taught him that he must listen to the God of Israel who created the world.

Find the account of the ten plagues in Exodus 7:19–12:30, and write them below in the proper order.

	Plague	Exodus Reference	Against Egyptian God(s)
1	Blood	7:20	Hapi—god of the Nile
2	Frogs	8:6	Heqt—god of frogs/fertility
3	Gnats	8:17	Geb—earth god
4	Flies	8:24	Scareb—god of eternal life
5	Livestock	9:3	Apis—black bull god
6	boils	9:8–9, 15	Priests—unfit to serve
7	hail	9:18	Isis/Osiris—rain gods
8	locust	10:4	Serapis—locust protection
9	Darkness	10:21–22	Ra—sun god
10	firstborn	11:5ff	

The plagues were miracles and would not have happened without God's intervention. Notice, however, how God worked within His created world, using the events and powers of nature. Also interesting is the fact that most of the plagues were attacks on Egypt's false gods.

For instance, instead of inventing strange creatures to torture Egypt, He used flies, frogs, and hail. The unusual number of frogs and flies and the size of the hailstones made these events miracles. Locusts had destroyed crops in Egypt before, but not everything.

Define *miracle*: event that conuid some super rison
power

Another strange thing happened to prove that these plagues were miracles. The Israelites lived next to the Egyptians, but only the Egyptians suffered from the plagues. God protected Israel while He punished Egypt. True miracles clearly show that some supernatural power is behind them.

THE PASSOVER

Jews today still celebrate the Passover feast. For many Jews it is their most important national and religious celebration. This feast began the night that God brought the last plague on Egypt—the death of every family's firstborn. That same night, Israel left Egypt. Every time the Jews celebrate Passover, they remember how God brought their forefathers out of Egypt.

Extra Assignment: After reading Exodus 12:1–16, write an essay describing the Passover feast in your own words. Tell what kind of lamb each family chose. What did they do with the lambs? What foods did they eat with the meat? How were they to eat them? Why was it called "Passover"?

One of Christ's names is the Lamb of God (Rev. 5:6–14). Paul calls Him the Christian Passover (1 Cor. 5:7). The Passover lamb and Christ have six things in common. Discover how Christ compares to the lamb by telling how Christ is described in the following verses:

Passover Lamb	Christ
Without spot or blemish	Hebrews 4:15 _with out sin_
Saved the firstborn by its blood	Romans 5:8–9 _w are snvo by his blod_

No bones broken	John 19:36	No bones will be broken
Chosen for the specific purpose of becoming a sacrifice	Romans 3:25	sacrifice for sin
Eaten completely or burned; none left to decay	Acts 13:37	His body did not decay
Killed during Passover	John 19:14–16	Jesus died during passover

THINK ABOUT IT

What would you have thought if you were an Israelite and Moses told you that your oldest child will die during the night unless you killed a lamb and put its blood around your door? I thought that was to crazy but I'd did it first in case.

EXODUS
GETTING ORGANIZED IN THE DESERT

GOD'S LAW FOR GOD'S NATION

Why did God give Israel the Law? Galatians 3 helps us understand God's purposes. According to verse 19, why did God give the Law? _____
_____ *transgression* _____

Verses 21–22 teach that God's promise of salvation is fulfilled through faith in Jesus Christ, not by keeping the Law. God gave the Law to reveal to His people that they are incapable of meeting God's standard of holiness and earning salvation on their own. The Law also seems to have been intended to order and govern Israel's society.

Read Exodus 20. Then, in the following space, summarize each of the Ten Commandments in one sentence. Memorize them.

1. _____ *Worship other gods* _____ (20:3)
2. _____ *Don't think about them* _____ (20:4–6)
3. _____ *Misuse the name of God* _____ (20:7)
4. _____ *People should work hard* _____ (20:8–11)
5. _____ *Glory Honor Your Parent* _____ (20:12)
6. _____ *No murder* _____ (20:13)
7. _____ *No cheating on your husband or wife* _____ (20:14)
8. _____ *No stealing* _____ (20:15)
9. _____ *Be nice to your Neighbor* _____ (20:16)
10. _____ *Don't covet anything* _____ (20:17)

A PLACE TO WORSHIP

Because the Israelites had grown to more than two million people, God had to organize this growing nation. He had to keep them together somehow. First, He gave them a law. His authority and the authority of His Word would unite them as a nation. But God also wanted to unite them spiritually. He wanted them all to worship Him together.

So God gave them a central place to worship. He told Moses how to build a tent, or tabernacle, that would serve as the place where all of Israel could come together to worship. The tent represented not only the unity of God's people but also the real reason for their unity—God. The tent represented God's presence among them. In a sense, it was God's house—the place where He lived in their camp. But God made it clear that He could not be contained by a tent. He is everywhere and anywhere.

What did this tent look like?

First, it was more than just a tent. God designed a courtyard area fenced in by a heavy curtain. The main entrance to the court and to the tent always faced the east. Only men were allowed inside the court to bring their family's sacrifices.

- In front of the tent stood a _wash_. The priests washed themselves and sometimes the sacrifices in this great tub of water. In front of the laver stood the bronze _alter_ where the priests offered sacrifices to God.

- Inside the tent were two rooms. The larger room, about 15 by 30 feet, God called the _Holy plce_. Only the priests entered this room and only after they had washed. A _lamp stnd_ with seven lamps lighted the room. These lamps were bowls of oil with wicks sticking out. The _lampstnd_ reminded the people that God's Word lighted their way and helped them to see the truth. The priests kept the lamps burning and supplied fresh bread for the _table of bre of otth_, P-18, which stood opposite the lampstand. The bread represented man's sharing a meal with God. It represented the fellowship of man with God because

2

God dwelt among His people. The priests received some of the bread as payment for their duties. They burned the rest on the altar as a sacrifice (Lev. 24:5–9).

- The ___altor oxine esa___ stood directly before the curtain that divided the two rooms. The ascent of its smoke and aroma represented the people's prayers ascending to God.

- The second room—15 feet wide, 15 feet long, and 15 feet tall—contained only the ___arK of Covenant___. Once a year, the high priest entered this room to sprinkle blood on the ark for the forgiveness of the people. No one else dared to enter the room because God promised to be present. This room where God met His people was called the ___Holy of Holies___.

Label the following items on the diagram of the tabernacle with the numbers.

1. courtyard entrance	**2.** Holy Place	**3.** Ark of the covenant	**4.** laver	**5.** Holy of Holies
6. table of the bread of the Presence (shewbread)		**7.** altar of incense	**8.** lampstand	**9.** bronze altar

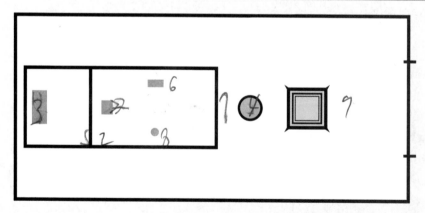

THINK ABOUT IT

Why do you think it is important that God planned for a place in the middle of the camp for His presence to dwell? ___His presence Hci. Important need with potin___

L E V I T I C U S

HOW ARE WE TO WORSHIP GOD?

God helped Israel organize not only the nation but also its worship. God appointed a special group of men called priests to lead in worship. The men came from the tribe of Levi. In the book of Leviticus, God instructed the priests how to guide Israel in worship.

Define *priest*: a levite who spoke of God for the people and offered their sacrifices

- Who became the first high priest of Israel? Aaron (Lev. 8:1–12; 21:10–24)

- How long did a high priest keep his office? until death (Deut. 10:6)

- Who became high priest after Aaron? Eleazar (Deut. 10:6)

WHOLLY HOLY

Decipher the code. Each letter below the blank stands for a different letter. Decode this statement and then find it in Leviticus.

B E	H O L Y	F O R	I	A M	H O L Y
Y V	S L O B	U L I	R	Z N	S L O B

Code clue: M=N and U=F

The main thought of this motto is found in several passages in Leviticus. Name them 11:44 19:2 20:26 21:8 .

The priests made themselves holy by dedicating themselves to God's service. They passed through a special ceremony in which they washed with water and made special animal sacrifices to God.

> Define *holy*: _devoted to God. set apart for specific purpose._

The tent of meeting became holy because it had a special purpose and was used only for that purpose. The same is true of all of its furniture and utensils.

To make and keep themselves and all of the articles of worship holy, the priests had to obey the laws of purity. Find some examples of these laws in Leviticus 21–22 and write them below.

21:1–4 close relatives – dies not shaving
7–13 days of marriage 22:1–3 no eating
sacrifices 4–6 no touching things unclean
given

How did God treat people who tried to worship Him without holiness (10:1–3)?

Kill offer offering fire strange fire
before Him

Holiness is still important to God. What does 1 Peter 1:16 tell us about holiness?

God say that we should be holy for He is
Holy

GIFTS FOR GOD

One way to worship God is to offer Him a gift. Did you ever have trouble buying a gift for someone because you didn't know what he liked or wanted? God told Israel exactly what He liked and wanted. By His law in Leviticus, they knew exactly what would be acceptable to God and what would not.

God called these gifts _offering_.

God told the Israelites He expected five kinds of offerings, each with a special purpose and meaning. Study Leviticus 1–6 and then list the name of each offering, describing what gift(s) was to be offered and the purpose of each offering.

Offering	Gift	Purpose
Burnt (1:1–17)	bull ram goat dove pig.	worship (1:9)
meat grain (2:1–16)	Grain worked Flour bread food Fo.	support priest praise god with 8r (2:10, 14)
Peace (3:1–17)	cattle sheep goats	thank God (7:12, 16)
sin (4:1-5:13)	god + Lamp dove pigeon (4:3, 23, 32; 5:7, 11)	confess ast to care (4:2–3; 5:5–6)
trepess Guilt (5:14–6:7)	ram	seeking forgive ness (5:15; 6:1–3)

These gifts meant nothing if the worshipper did not dedicate himself to God. They symbolized love, faith, and obedience. If a man made an offering just because he *had* to make an offering and did not care about worshipping God with his heart, God refused to accept his gift (Hos. 6:6).

- Who are priests in Christianity (1 Pet. 2:9)? christian

- What kinds of offerings do they bring to God (Heb. 13:15–16)? praise doing good, sharing

LET'S CELEBRATE!

God loves holidays! He commanded Israel to stop work and celebrate every seventh day. He gave them seven other celebrations for feasting and worship. Each event in some way celebrated Israel's special relationship to God. These holy days became holidays of rest. God allowed no work. By their feasting, singing, dancing, and relaxing, the people praised and thanked God for His love and care.

Find the eight holidays in Leviticus 23 and 25. List them and briefly describe what the people were to do on each Friday.

Feast/Holiday	Description
23:3 the Sabbath	7th day no work, but rest
23:4–8 the Passover and feast of Unleavened Bread	Passover must be ready, Unleavened Bread remember deliverance from egypt
23:9–22 Offering of the First fruit	deforestation of Harvest
23:23–25 the festival of trumpets	1st day 7 month no work assemble would gather

23:26–32	The Day of Atonement	(one day) 7th month, fasting, high priest w/ blood
23:33–43	the Festival of Tabernacles	live in tents for 7 days, remeber wandsei, in dessert
25:1–7	the Sabboth Year	every 9 years let the land rest
25:8–17, 39–43	the year of Jubilee	every 50! years no farming, freed slaves, freedom

THINK ABOUT IT

What do the painstaking details about God's plan for how His people were to worship Him reveal about how seriously we ought to take our worship? _____
___ God was serious then we should cann⊙___
_____
_____

N U M B E R S
MANNA AGAIN?

DECISIONS, DECISIONS

What did God command Moses to do in Numbers 1:1–3 and again almost forty years later in 26:1–2? _to number the people of Isreac especialls men over 20 who can fight_

What do you think this command has to do with the book's title?
Number os because it reports the cenres

The people of Israel made an important decision in Numbers 13:1–14:4. Weigh their decision on the table below. First, write the two recommendations from the different individuals. Next, write the reasons that were given for choosing between the two options.

Recommendation	Advocates	Reasoning
Don ot take the land	Ten spies and most of Israel	cities were fortified people where werson stronger
take the land	Joshua, Caleb, and Moses	land ox milk and hong, believe that God would help

Because the people made the wrong decision, God did not allow them to _have the land_. He made them wander in the _wilderness_ for nearly _40_ years until all of the adults had died, except _Caleb_ and _Joshua_ (14:29–31). The book of Numbers records the history of those forty miserable years of punishment.

Looking at the table, what should have made the difference in Israel's decision? _God should have been the difference_

SEE WHAT THE GROUCHIES GET YOU?

"Living in tents. Eating manna every day. Nothing but hot, dry desert. Sand in your eyes, in your clothes, and in your food. Slavery in Egypt was better than this!" That's how the Israelites felt during those forty years.

Read each of the following passages from Numbers and then list the Israelites' complaint in the first column and God's answer in the second column:

	Israelites' Complaint	God's Answer
11:1–3	Hardship hearing in the Lord	Fire
11:4–6, 31–34	only ate Manna	a plague and quac
14:1–4, 11–23	the flie is to Lon	He wanted to destroy them but Moses intercede
16:35–50	Complying to Moses and Aaron	a plague

Want to complain? Let it loose. List in the spaces provided four of your biggest gripes.

1. _my dad_
2. _rule_
3. _this_
4. _my dad_

Write Philippians 2:14 in the following lines:

Do everthing without grumbling or arguing

What do you think this verse means?

Do everthing without a fuse.

What do you think grumbling says about your satisfaction with what God has done for you?

I think grun being shoulds. exceesed

What do you need to change in your life to obey this verse?

stop my dad from arguing

THINK ABOUT IT

What does the outcome of the choice not to invade the land reveal about how important it is for us to believe that God will keep His promises?

I dant think

D E U T E R O N O M Y
IT'S TIME FOR A REVIEW

The wandering ended. The new generation of Israelites came to the border of Canaan. God had promised them the land. Finally they were about to receive it. They would not fail like their fathers and grandfathers, who had been afraid and did not trust God. Rather, they would take the land.

As Israel prepared to enter Canaan, God reviewed and explained His law.

Deuteronomy means ___Second___ law, or ___Law Repeated___.

Moses' duty as the lawgiver ended as this book ends. He also was forbidden to enter the Promised Land. So after bidding farewell, he climbed Mount Pisgah. There he viewed the Promised Land across the mouth of the Jordan River where it empties into the Dead Sea. There, under the care of God, Moses died.

GOD'S LAW FOR HIS PEOPLE

What did God tell Israel to do with His laws (Deut. 6:1–9)?

1. (6:3)	Obey as he can help you
2. (6:6)	to be on your heart
3. (6:7)	impress your children.
4. (6:7)	anytime, anywhere.

5.	(6:8)	*put on your body,*
6.	(6:9)	*write them on your Door way*

Read Matthew 22:38–40 and Deuteronomy 6:5. What did Jesus say was the greatest commandment? *to love God (with your...)*

Write out Deuteronomy 6:5 and memorize it. *Love the Lord, your God with all your heart and your soul and you love with all your strength*

A GREAT PROMISE

Moses said in Deuteronomy 18:15–19 that God would send a *Prophet* to Israel. This promise was fulfilled in two ways.

1. God used prophets to speak to His people. He no longer used the patriarchs. God's prophets reminded the people of God's Law. They spoke God's messages for the people of their day.

2. The Messiah became God's greatest prophet. God raised Him from among their brethren, just as Moses had predicted. Jesus was God's greatest spokesman. He revealed God's Word and even God Himself. (See John 12:49–50; Heb. 1:1–3.)

God also showed Israel how to tell a false prophet from a true prophet. According to Deuteronomy 18:20–22, what is the test of a prophet? *If he says is something that will happen*

THINK ABOUT IT

Why do you think the most important commandment is to love God with all that we are and have? *because especially be with him in all ways and obey he is God*

UNIT THREE:
THE PROMISED LAND

J O S H U A

GO GET 'EM!

CONQUEST

At last! They finally arrived.

For the second time, Israel stood on the bank of a body of water ready to cross at God's command. When was the first time? _red sea_ Israel had tromped eight hundred miles and aged forty years since then. Now they were camped by the Jordan River, ready to follow Joshua, their new leader, into the land that God had promised them.

What three promises did God make to Joshua in 1:1–5?

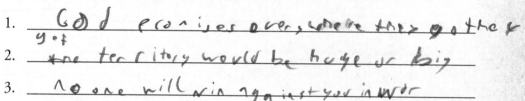

1. _God promises everywhere they gather got_
2. _the teritory would be huge or big_
3. _No one will win against you in war_

God said that He would give Israel the land of Canaan. The people living there already, the Canaanites, did not worship God. They worshipped idols. They did not respect God or His blessings. So God planned to annihilate them from the land to make room for His people.

God told Israel to fight for the land. They had to show that they trusted God by following His battle plans. God gave them the land free of charge, but they had to take care of it. First, they had to drive out the evil nations and destroy their idols.

Conquest of God's promised land began with Joshua's leadership. He wrote down a record of the conquest. That record became the book of Joshua, and it begins the historical division of Old Testament books.

What Scriptures did Joshua already have (1:8)? _the book_

of law

What did God tell him to do with these books (1:8)?

to keep it in meditate on it and obey it

Joshua needed strength and courage to lead Israel in conquering the land. What good reason did God give him for being strong and courageous (1:9)?

the lord your god will be with
you wherever you go

List some times when you need to be strong and courageous.

1. _covid-19 l now_
2. _loss of mother_
3. _going to college_

4. _____

What three things does Joshua 1:6–10 say that you can do to be strong and coura-geous like Joshua?

1. _7 one a day the bible_ .
2. _to obey all laws_ .
3. _the lord will be with you_

REMEMBER!

Two types of special/celebratory days are birthdays and holidays. Birthdays celebrate life by (1) remembering the day you were born and (2) honoring you on growing another year older. Holidays also celebrate by remembering special events and honoring people. Such special days are memorials. We have other kinds of memorials too—statues, buildings, plaques, and monuments. For example, the Washington Monument honors George Washington, reminding us of his leadership and honoring him on his achievements. What other memorials can you think of, and how do they remind and congratulate?

One men brial is in ge rm an where it is like a grace yard in the middle ox the city

Israel set up one memorial and celebrated two others upon entering the Promised Land. Find each in the following references and describe it. After telling what the memorial was, describe the event of which it reminded Israel.

THREE MEMORIALS IN JOSHUA

Memorial	Reminded Israel of...	Honored God by...
4:1–9 _monument of 12 stones from the Jordan River_	_God cutting of the flow of the Jordan so they could cross_	_giving thanks for the good lans_
5:1–8 _Circumcision_	_the people who server military_	_giving thanks tempteoy ve here_
5:10–12 _Passover_	_no more manna_	_giving their trist god leas them here_

ONE FOR YOU, ONE FOR YOU, ONE...

After Israel conquered Canaan, God divided the land among the twelve tribes. Land portions depended on the number of people in a tribe, the kind of land (hills or plains, dry or fertile), and the tribe's position in the nation. For instance, the tribe of Judah received the most prominent portion because Judah had inherited the birthright.

Levi's tribe received only cities scattered throughout all of the tribes. God gave the priests pasture land around the cities too. But God did not want them to have much land. He wanted them to have plenty of time to serve Him and His people. Not having land would free them of the work of caring for and tilling it, thereby giving time to serve the people.

Instead of Joseph getting a single portion, the tribes of Ephraim and Manasseh, Joseph's sons, each got a separate portion of land.

The tribe of Simeon received land within the allotment to Judah because the Judahites had more land than they needed.

Using a Bible atlas and Joshua 13, identify the territory assigned to each tribe and label it on the following map:

JOSHUA'S COVENANT

What promise did Joshua extract from the people in 24:14–24?

serve only God ng tivol

What memorial did Joshua give them in 24:25–27?

a stone to remind then of their
promise

Write Joshua 24:15 below. Memorize it.

But if serving the Lord seems
undesirable to the nchoose for yourself
this day whom you will serve w-other
the gods your ancestor, serve beyind
the Euenrats of the gods of the
Amorites, in whose land you are living. But
as for me and my household we will serve the Lord

THINK ABOUT IT

Why do you think it was so important for the Israelites to kill all the Canaanites?

Because they sinned badly

J U D G E S

GOING IN CYCLES

IF THERE WERE NO GOVERNMENT...

Describe briefly what you think your country would be like with no government.

It would be governmentless and be
barbaric.

For _____ years after the death of _Joshua_, God used _Judges_ to lead Israel. Unlike judges in our day, Israel's judges did more than make decisions about law enforcement. They _governed the people_ and _led the Army_.

God appointed these judges to _deliver Israel_ from _slavery_. He told them to _annihilate war_ and showed them how to _guide Israel in serving Him_.

But the judges did not have as much power as a king might. Many people paid no attention to the judges or their tribe's elders. What do you think the author of Judges (perhaps Samuel) is trying to tell us in 17:6; 19:1; 21:25 by repeatedly saying that in those days there was no king in Israel?

After all God had done for Israel, they still turned to _Idol worship_. They wanted a god they could see. Because they failed to drive out all of the _____ as God had told them to do, they were exposed to Canaanite gods and their rituals of false worship. They soon began to like the Canaanites and their gods of _stone_, _wood_, and _____.

65

Why did Israel's idol worship make God angry?

1. _____ Idol were not real, only 1 true God _____

2. _____ break 2 command and more _____
   _____

3. _____ God is jealous God _____

Nothing else deserves our worship. God alone is worthy of our worship and praise.

God punished His people each time they turned to idols. When they repented, God raised up judges to deliver them. But during times of peace, Israel fell in love with idols again. Notice the cycle that the Israelites kept repeating.

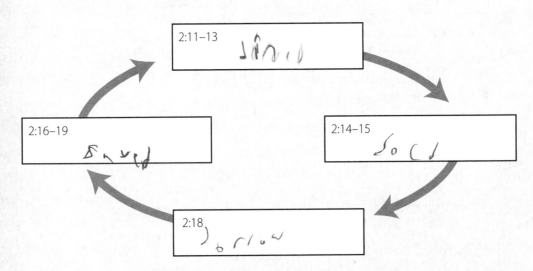

What does this cycle show us about the Israelites and ourselves?

• _____ He ign Jehova God _____
   _____

• _____ He get angr with Is _____
   _____

• _____
   _____

- _____
  _____

What does the cycle show us about God?

- He is a jeacoos God
  _____
- He yet angra wim prakstcaix
  _____
- He forgives again and again
  _____
- He loves us
  _____

FIND THE JUDGES

Find the names of the judges in the following verses. Then find them in the puzzle.

3:9	Othniel ✓	10:3	Jair
3:15	Ehud ✓	11:1	Jephthah
3:31	Shangur ✓	12:8	Ibzan
4:4	Deborah ✓	12:11	Elon
4:6	Barak ✓	12:13	Abdon
6:11	Ophrah	13:24–25	Samson
9:1, 22	Abimelex	1 Samuel 7:6	Shamgar
10:1–2	Issachar Tola		

Incomplete

```
S  H  A  N  G  E  E  L  O  N  Z  N  J  R  A
A  C  N  O  E  D  I  G  C  J  O  G  I  A  B
A  O  S  D  E  J  A  T  I  E  C  S  B  G  D
E  U  D  B  V  R  B  B  A  H  I  A  M  M  D
P  O  B  A  K  O  I  I  A  A  I  Q  U  A  O
H  J  E  P  H  M  M  I  Q  R  D  E  B  H  S
T  I  A  I  T  A  E  L  R  O  A  M  I  S  A
H  B  I  I  T  O  L  A  I  B  Z  K  A  I  M
A  Z  P  H  R  I  E  G  G  E  H  U  D  T  U
H  A  B  I  Z  K  C  Z  M  D  S  C  B  O  E
U  N  L  E  I  N  H  T  O  A  M  V  O  A  L
```

THINK ABOUT IT

Why do you think God kept delivering His people even though they constantly rebelled against Him?

Hes, people can live

R U T H

THE GOD WITH A PLAN

MATCH 'EM

Read the book of Ruth and then match the following characters and places to their descriptions:

D	1. Naomi	A. Redeemed Naomi's property and Ruth
H	2. Ruth	B. Naomi's husband
B	3. Elimelech	C. Naomi and Ruth returned to this town
G	4. Mahlon	D. Lost her husband and both sons
C	5. Bethlehem	E. Ruth's nation
A	6. Boaz	F. The tribe whose land included Bethlehem
F	7. Judah	G. Ruth's first husband
E	8. Moab	H. Met Boaz in a field

A MATCH MADE IN BETHLEHEM

What did Ruth promise Naomi (1:16)? Memorize that verse.

to never leave Her
_____
_____

How did Ruth keep her promise?

yes
_____
_____

A MATCH MADE BY GOD

Things looked bleak for Ruth after her husband died. Then Ruth discovered that God had a wonderful plan for her life. God's plan, however, went far beyond her imagination.

Ruth came from the country of Moab. She was not a Jew. Boaz's mother, _____Rahab_____ (Matt. 1:5), the harlot of Jericho, was also a Gentile. God used both women in His plan to bring the Messiah. According to Ruth 4:21–22 and Matthew 1:5–6, Ruth and Rahab became the great-grandmother and great-great-grandmother of King _____. Their most famous descendant was _____ (Matt. 1:16).

Use Ruth 4:21–22 and Matthew 1:5–6 to fill in the family tree.

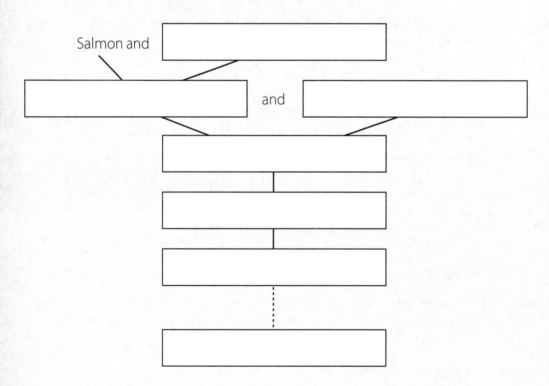

3 KEYS TO GOOD RELATIONSHIPS

1. _Be Faithful_
2. _Be Helpful_

3. _Be Kind_

BOAZ & CHRIST—RUTH & YOU

When Naomi wanted to sell her land, the law required that she let a relative of her husband buy back the land (Lev. 25:25). The closest relative had first rights to the land. He was called the kinsman redeemer (4:1–10). This law kept the land in the family. Israelites called it "redeeming the land."

> Define *redeem*: _to release from bondage_

According to custom, Naomi's kinsman redeemer gave his sandal to Boaz. This showed that he gave up his right to be the first kinsman redeemer. He wanted the land, but the law required that he take Ruth too (Deut. 25:5–10).

Boaz redeemed the land because he loved Ruth. He also wanted to help Naomi. When he redeemed the land, he also redeemed Ruth.

Christ bought you out of sin. You were born in bondage to sin, but Christ bought you back (redeemed you) with His own blood. Born a human, Jesus is related by blood to all men. He became our kinsman redeemer. (See 1 Cor. 6:19–20; Eph. 1:7–8; 1 Pet. 1:18–19.)

Do you think Ruth became a good wife to Boaz? Why or why not?

_____

_____

Boaz treated Ruth kindly. He bought Naomi's land so that he could help Naomi and marry Ruth. Do you think he was a good husband for Ruth? Why or why not?

_____

_____

_____

THINK ABOUT IT

Why is the book of Ruth in the Bible? What is so important about this story that God wanted it included in His Word?

__It is_____

_____

_____

_____

UNIT FOUR:
THE UNITED KINGDOM

I   S A M U E L

THE BOY WHO LEARNED TO LISTEN

IS ANYONE DOWN THERE LISTENING?

When _God_ speaks, I listen!

The second great prophet, Samuel (the first great prophet was _Moses_), became the last judge in Israel. The two books named after him begin a 450-year period of kings in the history of Israel. Samuel also began the great age of the prophets, which lasted until about 400 B.C.

Read 1 Samuel 1–3 to find the words to complete the following fill-ins:

- Elkanah had two wives, _Hannah_ and _Peninnah_, and he loved _Hannah_ very much even though she had not given birth to any children (1:1–5).

- Elkanah and his family worshipped at _Shiloh_, the city where the ark of God was kept (1:3).

- The high priest, _Eli_, thought that Hannah was _drunk_ when he saw her praying (1:9–14).

- Hannah prayed for _a son_ (1:10–11).

- Hannah promised that if God granted her request, she would _present the boy to God and never cut his hair_ (1:10, 22).

- Samuel was born to Hannah, served under _Eli_, and lived at _Shiloh_ (1:21–28).

- Eli's sons, _Hophni_ and _Phinehas_, abused their priestly privileges. A prophet told Eli that both sons would be punished and that they would _die on the same day_ (2:34).

- When Samuel heard _a voice calling his name_ in the night, he _ran to Eli_ (3:2–5).

- After this happened three times, Eli realized that _God_ was calling Samuel. He told the boy to lie down and if God called him again to say, "_speak Lord for your servant is listing_" (3:8–10).

- The Lord's voice surprised both Samuel and Eli because in those days the word of the Lord was _rare_ (3:1).

- God told Samuel that He would soon _punish Eli and his family_ (3:11–14).

- As Samuel grew up, all Israel recognized that he was a _prophet of the Lord_. God continued to _reveal_ Himself to Samuel (3:19–21).

WHAT'S THAT YOU SAY?

What three things did Samuel learn about listening?

1. Who: He learned to listen to the right speaker. To whom did he listen? _God_

2. How: He learned to stay still and be attentive. How did Samuel show that he was ready to listen? _he answered God and so still_

3. What: He learned to do something about what he had heard. Namely, he told others what God said.

   Whom did Samuel tell?
   - _Eli_ (3:16–18)
   - _Israel_ (3:20–4:1)

I can be a better listener in the following areas by:

- Who? _people that are higher than_
  Eli

- How? _by listing_

- What? _what th Rre saying and doing_
  that

THINK ABOUT IT

Why do you think Eli was willing to let his own sons defile the worship of God? How might people today be tempted to make the same mistake?

because the kren ie will got prnishd
by doing aregicing thing

I   S A M U E L
THE KING WHO NEVER LEARNED

Israel demanded a king. Samuel tried to persuade them to let God be their king. But they wanted to be like all of the surrounding nations with a king to lead them in battle and to meet with other kings and to govern them. The Lord gave in to their request. He instructed Samuel to give them a king—a man named Saul.

SAUL'S DIARY

What do you think Saul felt and thought of the strange things that happened to him? After reading each passage, complete the diary entry as you think Saul would have completed it.

I SAMUEL 9.1—10. 27

I never thought this would happen to me! A few days ago I went to look for my father's donkeys. When I couldn't find them, I went to ask Samuel the prophet for help. But he told me…

that I was important to come
but God governe a message

I SAMUEL 13.7—14

Today I did a stupid thing. We were getting ready to fight the Philistines. Samuel told me to wait for him at Gilgal, but…

now began burnt offering for
no reason. I am confidence.
where the came the soldier.
to dis obeying God

I SAMUEL 15:12—35

Samuel's not talking to me. He said God doesn't want me to be king anymore. I should have done what he said. We had a battle yesterday, and…

Samuel told to kill everything else except the king and some animals which I plan to to saraficed

I SAMUEL 18:1—19:10

I'm still king! Why don't they understand that? I'm king. Not David! After David killed Goliath…

the girl loved him and wanted him to be king and not me.

I SAMUEL 26:1—25

I was wrong about David. When I went out to kill him…

David came while I is sleep and took my spear and more and he could have kill me but he didn't

OBEDIENCE IS #1 WITH GOD

Saul's greatest failure was doing things his own way instead of obeying God. For example, he could not wait on Samuel and offered sacrifices himself (13:7–14). When God told him to kill every living thing among the Amalekites, including the cattle and the sheep, Saul killed most of them, but not all. He brought back Agag, king of the Amalekites, and some of the sheep and cattle alive (15:1–15).

Saul always had a good excuse for disobeying God's commands. When Saul returned from fighting the Amalekites, Samuel asked him why he did not kill all of the sheep and cattle. Saul replied, "We brought back some of the sheep to sacrifice to the Lord. The rest we totally destroyed."

"But you still disobeyed God," Samuel said. "To obey is better than sacrifice."

God wants us to obey. We might think that our way seems better. We might be bending God's rules only a little. We might even think that our way will bring more praise to God. But what God wants most from us is obedience.

Extra Assignment: Copy and memorize 1 Samuel 15:22.

But samuel replier: "Does the Lord delight in burnt offering and sacrifice, as much + obeying the Lord, To obey is better than sacrifice and to heed is better than the fat of rams

THINK ABOUT IT

What excuses do you make for failing to obey God? What does this reveal about the priorities of your own heart? Do you have idols of your own?

I have one idol: respect

L E S S O N   1 6
1   &   2   S A M U E L
1   C H R O N I C L E S
THE KING GOD LOVED

DAVID'S PLEASING HEART

God called David "a man after My own heart" (1 Sam. 13:14). God favored him because the thoughts and feelings of David's heart pleased Him. God told Samuel that man looks on the outward appearance, but the Lord looks at the heart (1 Sam. 16:7).

David became the greatest king Israel ever had. God loved him, and all Israel loved him because he was a king who was great in heart. King David cared deeply for God, a fact that is evident in the many psalms he wrote. He also cared for his people. He protected Israel with his life, leading the army into battle. He ruled with kindness and compassion.

Define *humility*: *putting the interest of others before yourself, accurate view of oneself*

Read each of the following Scripture passages and then summarize in the Event column what happened. Then, in the Character column, write what this shows about David.

	Event	Character
1 Samuel 16:6–13	*Samuel anointed David*	*God was with him*
1 Samuel 17	*David and Goliath*	*Pride and courage*

1 Samuel 18:5, 12–16, 30	Discression/ served fifth fully	Good leader
1 Samuel 18:17–19	David refused to marry Saul's daughter	humility
1 Samuel 20:16–23, 35–42	Jonthan warned David escape	Good friend
1 Samuel 24	David spared Saul	kindness
2 Samuel 6:12–22	David danced before the lod	Worship to God
2 Samuel 7:18–29	David prayed	trust in the Lord
2 Samuel 11:1–12:14	David sinned and repented	Confess before the lord

David wrote Psalm 51 to express his repentance for his sin with Bathsheba. Feeling sorry about our sin is not enough. After David felt sorry, he turned away from his sin and promised never to sin like that again. Read Psalm 51 and then define the word *repent* in the box below.

Define *repent*: to turn aways from sin to doing right

	Event	Character
2 Samuel 18	Absalom died	Loves his care is family
2 Samuel 24:18–25	David build an altar	willing to pay the price for serving the Lord

Jews today still consider David the greatest king who ever ruled. He expanded Israel's borders. He laid plans for a temple. He established peace. His greatest descendant, Jesus, came to this earth one thousand years later as the Savior of the world.

You might not be chosen by God to be a king like David, but you can be like him in your heart.

Unscramble the following key words to find out how you can be like David:

- I will be _brave_ (vebar) when giant temptations attack me.

- I will _love_ (olev) my _family_ (afymil) even when they are unkind to me.

- I will _love_ (vole) my _enemies_ (meeneis) and treat them _kindly_ (ylinkd) even when they hurt me.

- I will _worship_ (piorhsw) God with all my _heart_ (tareh).

- I will be a _faithful_ (ffiahutl) _friend_ (drinfe) to anyone who needs me.

GOD'S COVENANT WITH DAVID

Read 2 Samuel 7:1–17 and 1 Chronicles 17:1–15. Then answer the following questions:

What did David want to do for God (2 Sam. 7:1–5)?
to build a house of worship for
him

God did not allow David to do this, but He did make eight promises to David. Read the following verses from 2 Samuel 7 and then write out each promise:

1. Verse 9: _He will make David one famous_
2. Verse 10: _provide a place for Isreal_
3. Verse 11: _protec Isreal from the enemie_

4. Verse 12: _a son who will bruise great king_

5. Verse 13a: _a son will build the temple_

6. Verse 13b: _his kingdom will be established_

7. Verses 14–15: _God gave and disobey for his son_

8. Verse 16: _David's love, kingdom, and throne established for ever._

We have seen how God kept promises 1, 2, and 3. In the next lesson, we will see how God kept promises 4, 5, and 7. Read Isaiah 9:6–7 and Luke 1:32, and write how God kept promises 6 and 8.

His descendants, Jesus who will reign forever.

THINK ABOUT IT

What was David concerned about that made him willing to face the giant? (See 1 Sam. 17:45–47.)

_____

_____

_____

_____

I KINGS
2 CHRONICLES
THE KING WHO HAD IT ALL

MAKE A WISH!

If God said that He would give me anything I wanted, I would ask for…

a reality distructor

According to 1 Kings 1:28–40, which of David's sons became king after David died? _solomon_

When God promised the young king anything he asked, what did he choose to receive (3:4–9)? _wisdom (discerning heart)_

What did God give the king in addition to what he requested (3:10–15)? _abundant riches, honor, and long life_

What example of Solomon's wisdom does the writer of 1 Kings 3:16–28 give? _He discovered the truth, chose the true mother of the baby_

What books of wisdom did Solomon write? _Ecclesiastes, proverbs, song of solomon_

What dream of David's did Solomon accomplish in 1 Kings 5–8? _He built the temple of God_

SOLOMON'S GREATNESS AND DOWNFALL

Solomon had everything: wisdom, wealth, fame, and peace. He had more gold than any other king. He had seven hundred wives and three hundred concubines.

Solomon made silver and gold at Jerusalem as plentiful as stones (2 Chron. 1:15). He surpassed all the kings of the earth in riches and wisdom (2 Chron. 9:22).

His personal income was equivalent to about one half billion dollars per year. He owned 40,000 horses, 1,400 chariots, and a fleet of ships. His ivory throne overlaid with gold had six steps and a rounded back with armrests. Twelve lions surrounded it, two resting on each step.

Solomon had it all. Still he made mistakes. Why did God become angry with him in 1 Kings 11:1–13? What did he do?

He Married foreign woman fal bega anto
worshiptheir Gods

THINK ABOUT IT

How does the fall into idolatry by a man as wise as Solomon offer a warning about the tendencies of people's hearts?

keasy people sin

UNIT FIVE:
THE DIVIDED KINGDOM

Mediterranean Sea

Sea of
Galilee

Israel

Dead
Sea

Judah

LESSON 18
1 & 2 KINGS
2 CHRONICLES
KINGS AND KINGDOMS

THE BIG SPLIT

Read 1 Kings 11–12 and then complete the following statements:

Jeroboam rebelled against King _Solomon_ (11:26). The prophet _Ahijah_ predicted God would take away _10_ tribes from _Solomon_ and give them to _Jeroboam_ (11:29–31). But God allowed Solomon to die in peace. He did not lose part of his kingdom, but his son _Rehoboam_ did (12:12–20).

- What mistake did Rehoboam make in 12:1–17?
  He told the people that he would be tougher than Solomon. Chg

- What did the people of Israel do when Rehoboam refused to listen to them (12:16–20)? _Made Jeroboam king_

- Ten tribes followed Jeroboam. Levi's tribe was spread over Israel; therefore, Levites sided with both groups. Which tribe followed Rehoboam (12:20)?
  Judah

- What other tribe helped Rehoboam by supplying soldiers for his army (12:21)? _Benjamin_

- What mistake did Jeroboam make in 12:25–30?
  He turned idols very gods, creat o worship

WHO'S THE BOSS?

Read the following verses to create a list of the kings of Judah on the left and a list of the kings of Israel on the right in their proper order. Identify the eight good kings by putting a star by their names.

Judah	Israel
1 Kings 14:21 Rehobam	1 Kings 12:20 Jeroboam
1 Kings 15:1 Abijah	1 Kings 15:25 Nadab
1 Kings 15:9 Asa ☆	1 Kings 15:33 Baasha
1 Kings 22:41 Jehoshaphat ☆	1 Kings 16:8 Elah
2 Kings 8:16 Jehoram	1 Kings 16:15 Zimri
2 Kings 8:25 Ahaziah	1 Kings 16:23 Omri
2 Kings 11:3 (Queen) Athaliah	1 Kings 16:29 Ahab
2 Kings 12:1 Joash ☆	1 Kings 22:51 Ahaziah
2 Kings 14:1 Amaziah ☆	2 Kings 3:1 Joram
2 Kings 15:1 Azariah ☆	2 Kings 10:36 Jehu
2 Kings 15:32 Jotham ☆	2 Kings 13:1 Jehoahaz
2 Kings 16:1 Ahaz	2 Kings 13:10 Jehoash
2 Kings 18:1 Hezekiah ☆	2 Kings 14:23 Jeroboam II
2 Kings 21:1 Manasseh	2 Kings 15:8 Zechariah
2 Kings 21:19 Amon	2 Kings 15:13 Shallum
2 Kings 22:1 Josiah ☆	2 Kings 15:17 Menahem

2 Kings 23:31	Jehoahaz	2 Kings 15:23	Pekahiah
2 Kings 23:36	Jehoiakim	2 Kings 15:27	Pekah
2 Kings 24:8	Jehoiachin	2 Kings 17:1	Hoshea
2 Kings 24:18	Zedekiah		

Three kings of Judah brought revival, leading their people to turn from idols and to worship God. Find out who they were in the following passages; then put an "R" beside each of them on the preceding chart. (Hint: they should already have a star beside them because all three were good kings.)

- 2 Chronicles 17–20: ___Jehoshaphat___
- 2 Chronicles 29–32: ___Hezekiah___
- 2 Chronicles 34–35: ___Josiah___

During the time of the divided kingdom, what was the capital of...

- Judah (1 Kings 12:21)? ___Jerusalem___
- Israel (1 Kings 16:29)? ___Samaria___

What great evil did all of Israel's kings and most of Judah's kings commit?

___Idolatry___

THINK ABOUT IT

Why do you think it was so hard for the kings who did right before God to turn the hearts of the entire nation back to God?

___Because the people liked the king is wrong, swood over through him___

1 & 2 K I N G S
GOD'S MESSENGERS

What does an ambassador do? The President of the United States sends ambassadors to other countries because he cannot go himself. The U.S. ambassador to France, for example, represents our president and our country to the French government. He speaks for our government.

Similarly, a prophet is one who speaks in the place of another. God's prophets spoke to the people for God. A prophet did not inherit his office as a priest or king did. Rather, God appointed him, and the Holy Spirit empowered him.

During the divided kingdom, prophets preached mostly to the kings. They warned against idolatry. They predicted judgment. They advised kings on important decisions.

Two prophets dominate the pages of 1 and 2 Kings. God shows the power of His words by many miracles in their lives.

ELIJAH—GOD'S BAAL-BUSTER

Describe Elijah's contest with the prophets of Baal as recorded in 1 Kings 18:16–40.

Each prepare should sacrifice. The god who answers their request confirms should be considered the true God

Baalsent a fire. Elijah's God, sent fire that consumed everything

What unique experience did Elijah have that made him like only one other man in the Bible (2 Kings 2:1–12)? Who was that other man?

the other man was enoch

ELISHA—GOD'S MIRACLE MAN

Read 2 Kings 2–13 to discover seven of the sixteen miracles that Elisha performed. Write the Scripture reference in the first column and describe the miracle in the second column. Explain the purpose of the miracle in the third column.

2 Kings Reference	Miracle	Purpose
2:13-15	the water split	to separate the spirit way with
2:23-25	the bears came	Get his part told...
4:1-7	infinite oil	For a family to be happy
4:42-44	Feeding Hundr...	to feed one hundred men
5:1-19	heal a leper	bless his father
8:1-6	7-year famine ended	varied the money
13:20-21	man brought back from dead	power over death

OTHER PROPHETS

Other prophets also received and delivered messages from God during this time period. Read the following passages and write the name of the prophet whose ministry is described in each passage:

1 Kings 11:29–39: __Ahijah__

1 Kings 12:22–24: __Shemaiah__

1 Kings 22:7–28: __Micaiah__

1 Kings 19:5–7: __Isaiah__

2 Kings 22:14–20: __Huldah__

2 Chronicles 15:1–6: _Azariah_

2 Chronicles 16:7–9: _Hanani_

2 Chronicles 20:14–17: _Jehaziel_

2 Chronicles 20:35–37: _Eliezer_

2 Chronicles 35:25; 36:12: _____

THINK ABOUT IT

Although there are not people like the Old Testament prophets today, God has still given us people who explain His message to us as He revealed it in His Word. How is your attentiveness to that preaching similar or different to the Israelites' attentiveness to the message from God through the prophets?

_____

_____

_____

THE HARDEST LESSON EVER LEARNED

What's the hardest lesson you have ever learned? For me, it was the time in seventh grade when my friends and I broke a glass door at school. We told the principal, and he asked each of us to pay twenty dollars to replace the glass. He told us to tell our parents. I didn't. I decided to pay it secretly from my own money. But my brother had borrowed some money from me, and it would be a while before he could pay me back.

The other boys told their parents and brought in their money. For several weeks, the principal kept asking me about the money, and I kept putting him off.

I hardly thought about anything but that twenty dollars. I avoided talking to my parents. One night, my brother told Dad that I had broken a window at school. I denied it. "I was there," I said, "but I didn't do it."

Finally, my brother paid me back enough to make my savings total twenty dollars. I was going to give it to the principal the next day, but that same night the principal called my parents.

I got upset with myself for not telling my parents in the first place. The principal told me the right thing to do, but I had to learn it the hard way. That was the hardest lesson I learned in seventh grade.

God told Israel and Judah the right way to live, but both nations had to learn the hard way. They tried to find a right way on their own. They disobeyed and caused themselves a lot of pain and unhappiness. Finally, God said, "Enough!"

WHAT WENT WRONG?

Read 2 Kings 17:5–6, 18 to learn the final punishment that God brought on the northern kingdom of Israel. What was it?

_____

_____

Why did God bring such a harsh punishment on them (2 Kings 17:7–18)?

_____

_____

Who lived in Samaria after Israel was carried away captive (2 Kings 17:24)?

_____

_____

What happened to Judah about 136 years after Israel's fall (2 Kings 25:1–21)?

_____

Why did God bring about Judah's destruction (2 Chron. 36:11–16)?

- _____

- _____

- _____

- _____

- _____

How long did the prophets say the exile of Judah would last (2 Chron. 36:21)?

_____

THINK ABOUT IT

What evidence exists in your life that you are not guilty of the same sins as Judah? What evidence exists that you are guilty?

_____

_____

_____

_____

2 K I N G S
A FEW GOOD GUYS

In this unit we have been studying about a time period when most of the people "did evil in the sight of the Lord." However, there were a few good guys. In this lesson we will look at two of them, Kings Hezekiah and Josiah.

KING HEZEKIAH

Hezekiah pleased God because he…

- _____ in the _____ (2 Kings 18:5)

- _____ to the _____ (18:6a)

- Did not depart from _____ (18:6b)

- _____ the _____ that the _____ commanded _____ (18:6c).

So, God made him _____ in whatever he did (18:7).

Who sent a letter to Hezekiah (2 Kings 19:9–13)? _____

What did Hezekiah do about the letter (19:14–19)?

_____

_____

What else happened to King Hezekiah that made him pray? How was his prayer answered (2 Kings 20:1–11)?

_____

_____

_____

Have you ever prayed so hard that you cried? Hezekiah did. He prayed from his heart. Of course, he faced some desperate circumstances. Whether we are desperate or have a simple need, God wants us to pray from the heart.

God wants you to:

- _____

- _____

- _____

- _____

KING JOSIAH

What book did Josiah's men find (2 Kings 22:8)? _____

What two things did Josiah do when he heard the book read (22:10–13)?

1. _____
_____.

2. _____
_____.

What five things did Josiah do after the prophetess Huldah predicted destruction because Judah had ignored God's law?

1. 23:1–2: _____
_____

2. 23:3:_____
_____

3. 23:4: _____
_____

4. 23:21–23: _____
_____

5. 23:24: _____
   _____

God gave us a guide for our lives. We cannot let it gather dust in the closet. We need the Bible to tell us how to live. Knowing God's Word is the best way we have of knowing God.

How can we keep God's Word before our minds?

- _____
- _____
- _____
- _____

THINK ABOUT IT

What would have to change in your life for you to please God in the same way Hezekiah did? _____
_____
_____
_____

I hereby covenant with God to follow His Word. I will hide it in my heart. I will read it faithfully and consistently. I will study to show myself approved as God's workman. And I will apply it to my daily walk. Lord, help me to understand Your Word and Your will—and then to be faithful in obeying and practicing it daily.

Signature _____ Date_____

Note: Do not sign this covenant unless you intend to keep it. It is better to be honest than to make a commitment that you do not intend to keep. The most important question for you to ask is what your decision reveals about your heart. Your grade in class will not be affected if you do not sign.

UNIT SIX:
THE REMNANT KINGDOM

EZRA
GOING HOME

WHO?

The book of Ezra is named after its probable author, _____, a priest and scribe (7:1, 6). It tells how _____, king of _____, issued a decree that the _____ at _____ should be rebuilt (1:1, 3). He sent _____, son of Shealtiel, to govern the people and take charge of the construction (2:2; 3:2).

The book also tells how Ezra led a second group of exiles back to _____ from _____ (7:1–10). He came with a letter from King _____ (7:11), ordering him to teach God's law and restore proper worship in the temple. After the return, God's people became known as _____, the short form of Judeans (4:12).

WHEN?

Cyrus sent the first exiles back to Jerusalem in his _____ year as king of Persia (1:1). This was about ____ years after _____ had taken the first captives from Judah (2:1; 2 Chron. 36:21). God promised through Jeremiah that _____ would be destroyed after the 70-year captivity had ended (Jer. 25:12–14). The Babylonians were overthrown by the Persians (1:1).

Zerubbabel began rebuilding the temple in the _____ year after arriving in Jerusalem (3:8). Because of interruptions, the temple was not finished until the _____ year of King _____ (6:15).

WHAT?

When Zerubbabel's builders laid the foundation of the temple, some people
_____ and _____ (3:11). The older ones _____ because they
remembered how great and beautiful Solomon's temple had been (3:12). In contrast, the new temple looked humble and simple.

Two hundred years before Zerubbabel, God promised to save a _____
of Judah (2 Kings 19:30–31). He made this promise through the prophet
_____ to King _____ (2 Kings 19:20). God promised
that this _____ would _____ downward and
_____ upward in Jerusalem (2 Kings 19:30).

Judah's remnant was carried away to _____ (2 Chron. 36:20). God
fulfilled Isaiah's prophecy by bringing back _____
_____
_____ (Ezra 9:15).

Ezra became upset when he arrived in Jerusalem because _____
_____
(9:1–4). Ezra and the leaders decided to stop this sin and make the men repent by
_____
_____ (10:1–4).

Ezra asked the men to do two things (10:11):

1. _____

2. _____

THINK ABOUT IT

Why do you think it was important to deal so harshly with the men who had married foreign wives? _____

_____

_____

What does the book of Ezra reveal about God's grace and mercy? _____

_____

_____

What was God revealing about Himself when He promised a plan to redeem people in Genesis 3:15 and when He provided a way of deliverance for Noah and his family? _____

_____

_____

BUILDING GOD'S WALL; REBUILDING GOD'S PEOPLE

NEHEMIAH'S MISSION

Nehemiah lived in _____ (Neh. 1:1), about two hundred miles east of Babylon. (Locate it on a map.) Darius I built a palace there. The book of Esther describes it as a splendid palace that King Xerxes also used (1:1–7).

What was Nehemiah's job (Neh. 1:11–2:6)?

_____

According to 1:1, who wrote the book of Nehemiah? _____

What bad news did Nehemiah hear (1:2–3)? _____

_____

_____

NEHEMIAH'S PRAYER.

- He praised God for _____ (1:5).

- He confessed _____ (1:6–7).

- He asked God to _____ (1:6), to _____

  _____ (1:8–9), and to _____

  _____ (1:11).

Why do you think Nehemiah was afraid in the presence of King Artaxerxes (2:1–6; cf. Ezra 4:7–23; and Esther 4:11)?

- _____
  _____
  _____
  _____

- _____
  _____
  _____
  _____

What was Nehemiah's mission (2:5, 17)? _____
_____

REMEMBER.

Zerubbabel rebuilt the _____.

Ezra rebuilt the _____.

Nehemiah rebuilt the _____.

A LEADER IS...

Read the verses from Nehemiah, each section of which describes Nehemiah's leadership. Then see if you can unscramble the key words that tell us what made Nehemiah a great leader.

A LEADER IS A/AN...

2:17–18; 4:6		caoneergur
3:1–5		diornartooc
4:5–13		roarwir

4:13–18		renlanp
4:23; 5:14–19		nvertas
5:1–13	_____ of the weak	rfedni

IF YOU WANT TO LEAD LIKE NEHEMIAH…

1. _____ people to use their gifts for God.

2. _____ people work together.

3. _____ for God's truth.

4. _____ according to God's _____.

5. Be a _____ of others.

6. Be a _____ to the weak.

THINK ABOUT IT

What is surprising about Artaxerxes' reaction to Nehemiah, and how does it reveal God's power and His love for His people?

_____

_____

_____

E S T H E R
SAVED BY THE QUEEN!

Esther lived a few years before Ezra and Nehemiah. Xerxes (Ahasuerus) ruled in Persia then. Esther was born as an exiled Jew in Susa. She never saw Israel's homeland. Yet she saved all of the Jewish exiles from death, thereby allowing many of them to return to the Promised Land.

Esther's story was recorded in the records of the Persian kings (2:23; 9:20; 10:2), from which Ezra or another scribe may have copied part of the story. The writer may have been in Susa at that time and witnessed the events. Esther became famous among the Jews, and her story spread by word of mouth. The author may have heard and investigated these accounts of Esther.

GOOD GUYS AND BAD GUYS

Review the story of Esther. Then match the following list of descriptions with the correct names. All but one of the names have more than one description.

	1. Vashti	A.	Queen who refused to obey the king (1:10–12)
	2. King Xerxes (Ahasuerus)	B.	Hadassah (2:7)
		C.	Esther's cousin who raised her (2:7)
		D.	Married Esther (2:17)
	3. Mordecai	E.	Heard of assassination plan and sent word to the king through Esther (2:21–22)
	4. Haman	F.	Mordecai would not bow to him (3:2).
		G.	Influenced the king to issue a decree that all Jews should be killed (3:8–9, 12–13)
	5. Esther	H.	Bravely approached the king to ask him to save the Jews (7:3–4)
		I.	Hanged on a 75 foot (50-cubit) scaffold (7:9–10)
		J.	Ordered Jews to defend themselves (8:11)

WHEN GOD IS IN CONTROL

Mordecai encouraged Esther to be brave. Perhaps she could save the Jews by her courage. He believed that God had caused Esther to become Queen of Persia because He had a special plan for her. Perhaps that plan was to save Israel from Haman's death warrant.

Mordecai urged Esther to think about God's plan for her life. Read his words in Esther 4:12–14. What can you conclude that Mordecai believed about why Esther had become queen?

_____

_____

_____

Esther, Mordecai, and King Xerxes became part of God's plan to spare the Jews. God wanted to save the Jewish nation because He had promised that the Messiah would come from it.

God has a plan, and everyone has a place in that plan. God might not use you to save a nation as Esther did. Of the millions of Jews, only Esther was able to do that. But you fit somewhere in His plan. More than once in your life, you will be able to adapt Mordecai's words in 4:14 to your own situation.

God can and will use you to accomplish His purpose in the world. Will you, like Esther, be willing to do whatever He asks, no matter how hard it might be?

THINK ABOUT IT

What does the book of Esther reveal about God's sovereignty, purpose, and providence, even though He is not named in the book?

_____

_____

_____

_____

Extra Assignment: Write a paragraph telling about some event in your life that showed you that God had a plan for you or that God was working in your life. Then write a prayer, asking God to work in your life to use you to help others.

_____

_____

_____

_____

_____

_____

_____

_____

_____

_____

_____

_____

_____

_____

_____

_____

_____

_____

_____

_____

_____

_____

UNIT SEVEN:
POETRY

J O B

WHEN THINGS GO WRONG

The opening words of the book of Job describe how great Job became because he served God. God favored him and blessed him. Satan, however, saw him as the perfect victim for destruction.

THIS IS ONLY A TEST

God allowed Satan to give Job two major tests. Read Job 1–2 and describe each.

Test #1 (1:13–19)	Crssit foften? live, serven San, Baughters, Killed
Test #2 (2:7–8)	Crssof hea[th bois 9[Ɵ or the body

Complete the following statements:

Satan believed that Job would ___ 6 orse 6 od ___
if God's blessings were taken away (1:11; 2:5). Instead, Job __ vorshes __
__ Cod, did not sin os accusin god __ (1:20–22).

JOB'S QUESTION

Job's big question was, "Why?"

"Why is all of this happening to me?" Job cried. "I don't deserve this. I've lived my best for God." (See 7:20–21; 10:2–3; 13:20–27.) Job's wife and friends tried to answer his question and comfort him. They tried to advise him on a new direction for his life.

Summarize what each of the following people told Job:

- Job's wife

  Why Job suffered: he did not have the integrity he thought he had. That is, he was not as righteous and truthful as he claimed.

  What Job should do (2:9): _curse god and die_

- Eliphaz

  Why Job suffered (4:7–8): _He saved evil_

  What Job should do (22:23–25): _return to god, leave sin_

- Bildad

  Why Job suffered (8:13–14, 20): _He did evil, forgot god_

  What Job should do (8:5–6): _look to god, plead, live right_

- Zophar

  Why Job suffered (11:4–6): _Job is to righteous_

  What Job should do (11:13–15): _turn away's to god_

- Elihu

  Why Job suffered (33:29–30; 36:8–10): _God is correcting him._

  What Job should do (36:10): _repent his evil_

Why did Job refuse to accept their advice (31:4–6; 27:6)?

He was honest not perfect he lived righteous life

GOD'S ANSWER

Job had been questioning God. Now God questioned Job, and Job learned a great lesson from the questions. Read Job 38–39 and think about all the great questions that God asked Job. They reminded Job that God was the Creator, and Job was only one of His many creatures.

As your teacher explains the following points, listen carefully and write the three messages that God had for Job.

1. _Trust me Don't question_ (38:2; 40:2; 42:1–3)
2. _who are you to condemn me_ (40:8)
3. _suffering help you grow spirit_ (42:1–6)

What can you do to make it through the tough times like Job did?

1. _trust God_
2. _remember he has plan_
3. _God cares about you_
4. _look for ways to grow through trial_

THINK ABOUT IT

The book of Job does not tell us that Job ever found out about what happened in heaven—how God was making a point to Satan about how His servants feared and trusted Him. What lesson should we take from this book about how we respond to trials that we do not understand?

_____

_____

_____

SING IT!

You can fill in the following blanks by looking closely at Psalms:

- There are _____ (how many?) psalms.

- Psalms is divided into ___ books.

(List the psalms contained in each of these books. See the following example. Then look at the headings before the following psalms: 1, 42, 73, 90, and 107.)

Define *psalm*:

Book 1: Psalms _____

Book 2: Psalms _____

Book 3: Psalms _____

Book 4: Psalms _____

Book 5: Psalms _____

MEET THE COMPOSERS

- _____ is identified as the author of seventy-five psalms, including most of the psalms in Books 1 and 2. (See the headings to the psalms in these two books.)

- _____, David's choir director, wrote twelve psalms. (See the heading to Ps. 75.)

- The _____ wrote eleven psalms. (See the heading to Ps. 85.)

- _____ wrote two psalms. (See the heading to Ps. 72 and 127.)

- _____ and _____ wrote one psalm each. (See the headings to Ps. 88 and 89. See also 1 Chron. 15:17, 19; 16:42.)

- _____ wrote the oldest psalm. (See the heading to Ps. 90.)

- What is the total number of psalms composed by the preceding men? _____

- Subtract this number from one hundred fifty. How many psalms are anonymous? _____ These may have been written by David, one of the other named authors, or someone else entirely.

Extra Assignment: Write Psalm 1 on a clean sheet of paper as neatly as possible. Hang it on your bulletin board at home or on your mirror—some place you will see it often. Read it whenever you see it. Doing so will help you memorize it.

BIG IDEAS IN THE PSALMS

Six major themes are found throughout the psalms. As your teacher tells you what they are, write them in the following blanks:

1. _____

   In what four ways does Psalm 100 say that we can praise God? (See especially verses 1, 2, and 4.)

   _____
   _____

   Read these praise psalms: 66, 117, and 150.

Define *praise*:

2. _____

   According to Psalm 52:8, in what is David trusting? _____

   Read Psalms 31, 91, and 115 and note the writer's trust in God.

3. _____

   Write Psalm 103:8: _____

   _____

   Does God treat us as we deserve (103:10)? _____

   According to Psalm 103:12, what does God do with our sin when He forgives us?

   _____

   _____

   Read more about God's mercy in Psalm 32.

4. _____

   List five of the many things for which Psalm 136 thanks God.

   • _____

   • _____

   • _____

   • _____

   • _____

   Read Psalms 34, 75, and 118, and use them as thanksgiving prayers.

5. _____

   What does God's Word do for us (119:105)?

   _____

   Find out how valuable God's Word is by reading Psalm 1:1–3; 19:7–11; 119:9–16, 89, 129–130.

6. _____

Psalm 46:1–2 says that no matter what happens, God will be our _____ and _____ and give us _____ in times of trouble.

See how God saves by reading the following: Psalm 3; 18:1–19, and 144:1–11.

THINK ABOUT IT

List one way for each of the six big ideas in the Psalms that you can apply that idea in your own life.

_____

_____

_____

_____

_____

P R O V E R B S
A BIT OF WISDOM

Define *proverb*:

The book of Proverbs is a collection of wise sayings, most of which were written by _____ (1:1) to his _____ (1:8).

Proverbs is divided into the following five sections:

Chapters	Section

THE KEY TO WISDOM

Wisdom is the main subject of Proverbs. Solomon answers such questions as: How do I get wisdom? How can I keep it? What do I do with it?

Write Proverbs 1:7. _____

_____

_____

According to this verse, what is the first step on the road to wisdom?

_____

What does this mean? _____

Find the demands and benefits of wisdom in Proverbs 3:1–6. The demands are what Solomon tells us to do. The benefits are the promises that God makes about wisdom.

Demands	Benefits
Keep My commandments.	long life

Extra Assignment: Copy and memorize Proverbs 3:5–6.

_____
_____
_____

WORDS OF THE WISE TO THE WISE

How do I get wisdom (Prov. 2:6; James 1:5)?

_____
_____

What will wisdom do for me (Prov. 4:6–9)?

_____
_____

Extra Assignment: Choose a topic from the following list. Using a concordance and a topical Bible, find as many proverbs as possible on that topic. Group similar verses together, such as verses that repeat or give the same idea as another. Make a list of these verses and briefly note what each verse says about this topic.

- anger
- the fool
- pride
- joy
- friends
- money
- knowledge

- peace
- speech/the tongue
- worry/faith
- evil
- discipline/laziness
- immorality
- prosperity/security

THINK ABOUT IT

In which of the above topics from Proverbs do you most need to apply wisdom to your own life? Explain how. _____

_____

_____

_____

_____

E C C L E S I A S T E S
WHAT'S LIFE ALL ABOUT?

The title "Ecclesiastes" means "the preacher, the teacher, or one who addresses the assembly." (See its use in Ecclesiastes 1:1, 12.)

This preacher, a son of David and king of Israel after him (1:1), was _____.

The first words of the preacher present the problem about which he intends to write. The Preacher says that all things are _____ (1:2).

What does "vanity" or "meaninglessness" mean? _____
_____

SOLOMON'S QUESTIONS ABOUT...

Examine the following verses. Tell what things the preacher describes as meaningless.

1:12–18	4:13–16
2:1–11	5:8–17
2:17–26	

SOLOMON'S ANSWERS

Solomon does not give up just because life seems to have no meaning. He knows the source of meaning. It cannot be found in things or in man himself. It can be found only in God.

Solomon's most important answer is found at the end of the book in 12:13. According to this verse, what is the final word on the whole matter?

_____

_____

Solomon finds two other answers to the questions about life's meaning. See if you can find them in the following passages:

- _____ (2:24–25; 3:12–13)

- _____ (7:11–12, 19; 9:17–18)

Solomon does not suggest throwing out all of these things about which he complains. He suggests using them properly. Use them in light of God's coming judgment. Use them according to God's guidelines. Realize that they are temporary. Enjoy them, but don't make them a god.

GOOD TIMING

In Ecclesiastes 3:1–8, Solomon tells us how important timing can be in bringing meaning to our lives. Believers need to recognize that their purpose in life and their feelings of contentedness should not be controlled by their circumstances. God uses different circumstances—sometimes uncomfortable or painful circumstances—to draw the attention of His people to Himself and to make them more holy. Read the passage and see if you can think of an example of each time or season he talks about in those verses and how God might be using that season in your life to change you.

_____

_____

_____

_____

_____

ONE MORE THING TO MAKE YOU HAPPY

According to Ecclesiastes 4:9–12, what things bring meaning to life because they bring strength and love?

_____

_____

_____

THINK ABOUT IT

Why do you think the whole duty of man includes fearing God?

_____

_____

_____

S O N G   O F   S O L O M O N
A LOVE SONG

Write Song of Solomon 1:1. This opening phrase means that this song is the greatest and most beautiful of all songs.

_____

_____

It is a _____ song. It is sung between a _____ and his _____.
The lover is _____, and the beloved is _____
_____ whom he married (see 6:13). The song is about _____
_____.

Both Solomon and his bride describe _____
_____. Each tells how much he or she
_____. The bride becomes
afraid when she is _____ and
cannot find him anywhere.

Love in marriage takes the following three forms. Each is described in the song.

- _____ (1:2–3, 9–11, 15)
- _____ (3:1–4; 4:9–10)
- _____ (2:3–4; 8:6–7)

Solomon's song praises God's creation of married love. The book is a beautiful picture of the wholehearted commitment and devotion that God intends to be present in marriage. The key verses of the book are 8:6–7. In the space below, identify what you think are the key words in these verses and what they suggest about the main point of these verses:

_____

_____

_____

_____

_____

_____

THINK ABOUT IT

How is the message about love in Song of Solomon different from the messages about love that are in the world today?

_____

_____

_____

_____

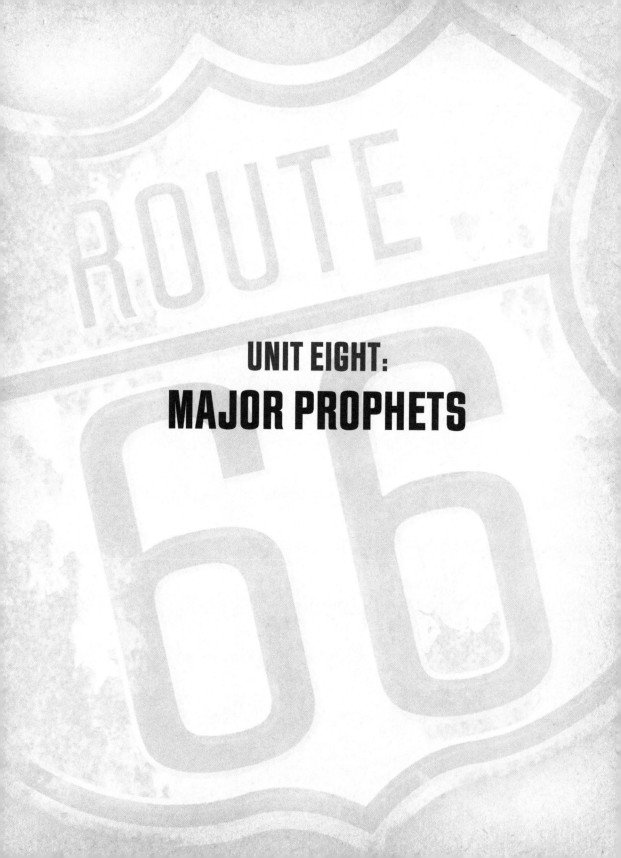

UNIT EIGHT:
MAJOR PROPHETS

ISAIAH

HE'S COMING

Isaiah prophesied to the nation of _____ during the reigns of _____, _____, _____, and _____, kings of _____.

During his life Isaiah saw the northern kingdom carried away into slavery. He warned Judah that it would also be enslaved because the people did not keep away from _____ (2:8–9).

Isaiah promised the return of a _____ of God's people (10:20–22). He also proclaimed God's promises about the coming of a great _____ and His _____ (9:6–7). This would be the Messiah.

Define *Messiah*:

ISAIAH'S MISSION

Read Isaiah's call to service in Isaiah 6:1–13. Then answer the following questions:

- When did Isaiah have this vision (6:1)? _____

- What did Isaiah see (6:1–2)? _____

- What did the seraphim call out (6:3)? _____

- What did the sound of their voices cause (6:4)? _____

- How did Isaiah feel when he saw and heard these things (6:5)? _____
  _____

- What did one seraph do to help Isaiah (6:6–7)? _____
  _____

- According to the seraph, how did this help Isaiah (6:7)? _____
  _____

- What question did the Lord ask (6:8)? _____
  _____

- What did Isaiah do when he heard the question (6:8)? _____
  _____

God told Isaiah to go speak to a people who would not listen. "They will reject you," God promised him. "They will hear, but not listen. They will see, but not understand what it means. They are very stubborn."

ISAIAH'S MESSIAH

Read the following nine prophecies in Isaiah. Tell what each predicts in the Prophecy column. Tell how each came true in the Fulfillment column, using the New Testament references.

Isaiah	Prophecy	New Testament	Fulfillment
7:10–14		Matthew 1:18–23	
9:6–7		Luke 1:32–33	
28:16		1 Peter 2:4–6	

35:5–6		Luke 7:20–22	
53:4–6		Matthew 8:16–17; 1 Peter 2:24–25	
53:7		1 Peter 2:23; (Acts 8:32)	
53:9		1 Peter 2:22; Luke 23:32–33, 50–53	
59:16–21		Galatians 3:13–14	
61:1–2		Luke 4:16–21	

Extra Assignment: Write out and memorize Isaiah 53:5–6.

_____

_____

_____

_____

THINK ABOUT IT

Why do you think Isaiah fell on his face when he saw the vision of God in Isaiah 6? How can you demonstrate Isaiah's attitude today?

_____

_____

_____

J E R E M I A H
L A M E N T A T I O N S
STAND UP!

A MAN CALLED JEREMIAH

Read Jeremiah 1. Then circle the correct answers below. Circle only one answer unless otherwise noted.

Jeremiah prophesied to the southern/northern kingdom of Judah/Israel (1:2). He saw five kings on that kingdom's throne. Circle the correct five (1:2–3; see also your list of kings in Lesson 18).

Hezekiah	Josiah	Jehoahaz	Jeroboam
Jehoiakim	Jehoiachin	Ahab	Zedekiah

Jeremiah was the son of a priest/prophet in Jerusalem/Anathoth (1:1). He had a scribe named Benjamin/Baruch who wrote God's words through Jeremiah's dictation (36:4).

JEREMIAH'S ASSIGNMENT

God began planning Jeremiah's special assignment before _____ (1:5). Jeremiah said he couldn't_____ because he was so _____ (1:6). But God told him not to be afraid because _____ _____ (1:8). God appointed Jeremiah as a _____ (1:5).

In 1:17–19, God ordered Jeremiah to stand up and stand strong. He promised to help keep Jeremiah strong. List three objects to which God compared Jeremiah in verse 18. Tell how each object illustrated God's strength in Jeremiah.

1. _____

   _____

   _____

2. _____

   _____

   _____

3. _____

   _____

   _____

A CRY BABY?

Jeremiah lived in an unhappy time. He watched Josiah's revival fade. He saw Jerusalem invaded by foreign armies four times. The final invasion completed the destruction of the temple and the city wall. Judah's last four kings hated him, as did the priests, the false prophets, and the leaders of Jerusalem. They beat him and put him in stocks (20:1–3). They tried to kill him (26:7–9). He was thrown into a dungeon in prison (37:11–16). They put him into a muddy cistern (38:6).

Once Jeremiah dictated a prophecy that Baruch wrote on a scroll. Baruch read it to the people. When King Jehoiakim heard about the scroll, he cut it up and burned it. God told Jeremiah to write the scroll again, so he did (36:1–32).

Jeremiah sometimes felt depressed because everyone rejected him. Look at his complaint to God in 20:7–8. According to verse 9, what answer did he discover?

_____

_____

Jeremiah cried not only about his own problems but also about the terrible things the Jews brought on themselves by their disobedience. Therefore, Jeremiah is often called the "weeping prophet." He described his tears in 9:1.

LAMENTATIONS

After the destruction of Jerusalem, Jeremiah wrote Lamentations, a poem lamenting the city's death.

In that book he compared Jerusalem to a _____ who had lost everything. She was once a _____ (queen) among the provinces but had now become a _____ (1:1).

What three reasons does Jeremiah give for Jerusalem's fall?

1. Lamentations 1:8–9: _____
   _____

2. Lamentations 4:11–12: _____
   _____

3. Lamentations 4:13: _____
   _____

But the book is not all sadness. What characteristic of God does Jeremiah praise in Lamentations 3:22–33? _____

Jeremiah advises Jerusalem's citizens to _____
_____ (3:40–42).

THINK ABOUT IT

If someone were writing a lamentation about your life, in what ways would the author be able to lament your failure to repent and ask God's forgivenenss?

_____
_____
_____
_____

EZEKIEL
GOD'S ACTOR

INTRODUCING THE CAST

While Jeremiah prophesied in Jerusalem, Ezekiel preached in _____ , a city near the _____ River in the land of the _____, which is more commonly known as Babylon (1:3; 3:15).

Use a Bible dictionary and the following verses to discover…

- How Ezekiel came to Tel-abib (1:3; 2 Kings 24:14–17):

  _____

  _____

  _____

- His profession (1:3):

  _____

- Why he started prophesying (3:16–21):

  _____

  _____

- His main message (33:10–20):

  _____

  _____

  _____

GOD'S WATCHMAN

According to 3:17–21 and 33:1–9, what three responsibilities do God's watchmen have?

1. _____

2. _____

3. _____
   _____

Jesus Christ makes every Christian an _____ (2 Cor. 5:20). We are sent out to represent Him in the world. We are sent out to be His watchmen.

I can be a watchman by:

1. _____

2. _____
   _____

3. _____

SCENES 1–10

As we began our study of the Bible, we learned that God communicates to people in two ways: words and actions. God gave Ezekiel words to speak. He also used actions in a special way to speak through Ezekiel.

God asked Ezekiel to perform ten dramas that symbolized prophecies. Read the following references and tell briefly what Ezekiel was told to do and what each drama symbolized:

Text	What God Commanded Ezekiel to Do	What It Symbolized
4:1–3		
4:4–5		
4:6–8		

4:9–17		
5:1–12		
12:1–16		
12:17–19		
21:6–7		
21:18–24		
24:15–27		

THINK ABOUT IT

How has your life demonstrated the reality of repentance—in your actions, not just your words?

_____

_____

_____

_____

_____

DARING DANIEL

MULTIPLE CHOICE

Read Daniel 1–3. Then choose *all* of the correct responses to each of the following statements. (Some of them might have more than one correct response.)

	1. Daniel came to Babylon because (1:1–6):
	a. He wanted a vacation. b. He was running away. c. Nebuchadnezzar brought him. d. God told him to preach there.

	2. Daniel was chosen to be educated in the palace because (1:3–6):
	a. He interpreted the king's dream. b. He came from a royal family. c. He was smart and handsome. d. He qualified to serve in the king's palace.

	3. Daniel's friends' names were changed to (1:6–7):
	a. Larry, Moe, and Curly. b. Shadrach, Meshach, and Abednego. c. Hananiah, Mishael, and Azariah. d. Jehoiakim, Jadez, and Belteshazzar.

	4. Daniel and his friends (1:8–20):
	a. Grew stronger, wiser, and healthier than the other trainees. b. Were placed in the king's service. c. Were sent to Jerusalem. d. Liked green eggs and ham.

5. The king ordered all of the wise men put to death because (2:1–13):

a. None of them could describe and interpret his dream.
b. Some of them would not bow down to him.
c. They predicted he would lose a battle and be killed.
d. They brought home bad report cards.

6. Daniel told Nebuchadnezzar (2:26–28):

a. No one could interpret the dream.
b. He could interpret the dream.
c. Only God could interpret the dream.
d. God gave him the dream.

7. Nebuchadnezzar dreamed about (2:31–35):

a. A large, dazzling statue.
b. Being chased by killer cows.
c. Seven lean cows eating seven fat cows.
d. Being dethroned.

8. Nebuchadnezzar made a gold image and declared (3:1–6):

a. "Throw away all of your other gods and worship only this image."
b. "When you hear the music, worship this image."
c. "Whoever touches the statue will have his fingernails peeled off."
d. "Whoever does not bow down to this image will be thrown into a blazing furnace."

9. When Shadrach, Meshach, and Abednego refused to worship the image, Nebuchadnezzar (3:8–29):

a. Got mad.
b. Gave them a second chance.
c. Had them thrown into a blazing furnace.
d. Made them eat raw chicken livers.

DARING DEEDS

Read in chapter 6 how Daniel dared to oppose one king to serve another king. God tested Daniel's courage to the limit. What made Daniel so brave and firm in his commitment to worship God alone?

- 2:16–23; 6:10: _____

- 2:27–28; 6:23: _____

- 1:8; 6:4–5, 22: _____

NEBUCHADNEZZAR'S DREAM OF A STATUE

Read about Nebuchadnezzar's dream in 2:29–45. He saw a symbolic statue in the dream. Fill in the descriptive chart of the statue. On the left-hand side, tell of what material each body part was composed as explained by Daniel in verses 31–35. On the right-hand side, write the interpretation—that is, what each part stands for. In addition to verses 36–45, you will need a study Bible with notes or a commentary to complete the interpretation.

Dream	Material	Interpretation
head		
chest & arms		
belly & thighs		
legs		
feet		

Daniel saw that the stone that topples the statue will be a kingdom set up by God that will grow into a great mountain. This is the kingdom of God about which Jesus taught. The kingdom over which Jesus reigns will never be destroyed. It will endure forever.

THINK ABOUT IT

According to Daniel 1:8–21, why did Daniel succeed? What caused the chief of the eunuchs to grant Daniel's request, and why did he and his friends grow in knowledge and skill?

_____

_____

_____

_____

_____

UNIT NINE:
MINOR PROPHETS

H O S E A
THE GOD WHO IS ALWAYS FAITHFUL

HOSEA

Prophet to: _____

Period: _____

Historical notes:

- Israel went into _____ during his lifetime.

- He prophesied concerning the fall of _____ , Israel's
  _____ .

Message: God's love is _____. _____ and _____ to
Him.

A SYMBOLIC FAMILY

God commanded Hosea to marry a wife of _____ (that is, a prostitute; a woman not committed to any one man—1:2). Hosea chose _____
(1:3). She represented the adultery of Israel (1:2; 4:1, 12). Hosea represented
_____, who loved Israel in spite of her sins. He made the Israelites His people in
spite of their desire for _____ (4:17).

Name Hosea's children. Tell what each name means and what each name prophesied according to these verses:

- _____

  (1:3–5): _____
  _____

_____

_____.

- _____

(1:6–7): _____

_____

_____.

- _____

(1:8–11): _____

_____

_____.

Gomer left Hosea to become a prostitute again. What does Hosea do in chapter 3?

_____

_____

GOD'S STUBBORN LOVE

What a wonderful picture of God's stubborn love! Just as Hosea was faithful to unfaithful Gomer, so God was faithful to unfaithful Israel. God gave Israel opportunities to repent, yet Israel committed spiritual adultery by going to other gods.

Hosea's purchase to redeem his wife portrays the purchase God made 750 years later. God loves the people He created, but everyone has sinned (Rom. 3:23). Everyone has turned away to other gods, especially the god of self. But God bought His people out of slavery to sin. The price was Jesus' blood (1 Pet. 1:18–19).

Hosea did not give up on his wife. He found her, bought her, and brought her back home. He loved her even after she left him. God keeps on loving us, even when we return to sin. He forgives us again and again (Matt. 18:21–22; 1 John 2:1–2).

ISRAEL'S ONLY HOPE

- What answer to the spiritual adultery in Israel does Hosea propose in 6:1?

  _____

- In 6:6? _____

- In 10:12? _____

  _____

- In 14:1–2? _____

What hope does Hosea give to Israel in 14:4–9?

_____.

How can this book, especially chapter 14, encourage backsliding Christians today? (A backslider is one who strays from his commitment to Christ.)

_____

_____

THINK ABOUT IT

What does this book reveal about God's forgiveness and mercy?

_____

_____

_____

_____

J O E L
GOD'S AWESOME PROPHET

JOEL

Prophet to: _____

Period: _____

Historical notes:

- Prophesied during a severe _____

- Name means _____

Message: God will _____ and _____. Prepare for the _____
_____.

What disaster in Judah does Joel say illustrates God's coming judgment (1:2–7)?

_____

THE AWESOME DAY

What special day is coming in Judah (2:1, 11)?

_____

What do the locusts symbolize (2:3–11)?

_____

Another special day is prophesied in 3:1–17. Who is to be judged on that day (3:2)?

_____

THE AWESOME CALL

In Joel 2:12–17, Joel calls the people to repentance. According to the following verses, what does He command them to do?

- Verse 12: _____
  _____

- Verse 13a: _____

- Verse 13b: _____

- Verses 15–17: _____
  _____

What reason does Joel give for repentance in 2:13–14?

_____
_____

THE AWESOME PROMISE

From the following list, check (√) the promises found in Joel 2:18–32. Leave blank the promises not found in this passage.

- ☐ Jehovah will drive His people from the land.

- ☐ Jehovah will send grain, wine, and oil.

- ☐ Jehovah will send rain.

- ☐ Jehovah will drive away Judah's enemies.

- ☐ Jehovah will rescue His people from locusts.

- ☐ Jehovah will bless the crops.

- ☐ Jehovah will give His Spirit to all people.

- ☐ Jehovah will save all who call on Him.

- ☐ Jehovah will raise up a king.

According to Peter in Acts 2:15–21, when did the prophecy of Joel 2:28–32 begin to be fulfilled? _____

READY OR NOT...

- "Prepare!" Joel cries. "Prepare for the Day of the Lord." What special day will this be for our time?_____

- According to 2 Peter 3:14, 17–18, what can we do to prepare for the day?

  - _____
    _____

  - _____
    _____

  - _____
    _____

THINK ABOUT IT

How do you need to be preparing for Christ's return and the Day of the Lord?

_____
_____
_____
_____

AMOS
PREPARE TO MEET YOUR GOD

AMOS

Prophet to: _____

Period: _____

Historical note:

- Preached to _____ as well as Israel

Message: Prepare to _____. Repent. Put away _____ and treat all people _____.

TO WHOM IT MAY CONCERN

Amos was a _____ of Tekoa (1:1). He prophesied to the following cities and nations:

- _____ (1:3–5)

- _____ (1:6–8)

- _____ (1:9–10)

- _____ (1:11–12)

- _____ (1:13–15)

- _____ (2:1–3)

- _____ (2:4–5)

- _____ (2:6–16)

For each nation, Amos predicts that God will not turn back His _____ because of their _____. Although he speaks of each nation, Amos addresses his message to the northern kingdom.

SO WHAT DID WE DO?

"Prepare to meet your God," Amos declares (4:12). It will be an embarrassing meeting, he says. Israel is guilty. God is coming to judge them.

Of what sins does God accuse Israel in the following passages?

- 2:6–8; 4:1: _____

- 4:4–5; 5:26 (Hint: Bethel and Gilgal had high places for idol worship. God is speaking sarcastically here.): _____

- 6:1–6:_____
  _____

- 6:8: _____

- 8:4–6: _____

SO WHAT'S WRONG WITH OUR RELIGION?

How did God feel about Israel's worship? Why (5:21–26)?
_____
_____

Do you think God is sometimes unhappy with our worship? If so, when?
_____
_____
_____

From this passage (and the prophets generally), we learn what makes our worship acceptable to God. Christians find these same ideas taught in the New Testament. In the following verses, discover how you can make God happy through your worship:

Romans 12:1: _____

_____.

John 4:24: _____.

John 14:6: _____

1 John 2:3–6; 5:2–5: _____

THINK ABOUT IT

What is the difference between the ritual of your worship and the genuine worship Amos calls for? _____

_____

_____

_____

J O N A H

THE BIGGEST FISH STORY

JONAH

Prophet to: _Nineveh_

Period: _divided Kingdom_

Historical note:

- Nineveh was the _capital_ of the _Assyria_ empire.

Message: God will _Judge_ and _save_. Prepare for the _Day_ of the Lord. God cares about all _Nations_ .

SOMETHING FISHY

If you think you know the story of Jonah, try the following true/false statements without looking at your Bible. Use a pencil. Then go back and look up the ones that sound fishy. Use a pen to circle your final answers.

☐ T | ☒ F   1. The Lord commanded Jonah to go to the city of Tarshish and cry against it.

☐ T | ☒ F   2. Jonah traveled to Joppa where he boarded a ship to flee God's presence.

☐ T | ☒ F   3. The sailors prayed to the Lord when the wind made the sea rage.

☒ T | ☐ F   4. Jonah asked to be cast overboard to calm the sea.

☐ T | ☒ F   5. Jonah spent forty days and nights in the great fish.

☐ T | ☒ F   6. Jonah prayed from within the great fish that he would die instead of having to go to Nineveh.

☒ T | ☐ F   7. The Lord spoke to the fish, causing it to spit up Jonah on dry land.

☐ T | ☒ F   8. Having received the command again, Jonah attempted to flee in another direction.

☒ T | ☐ F   9. Jonah prophesied that the city would be destroyed by fire from heaven in forty days.

☐ T | ☒ F   10. The people of Nineveh laughed at Jonah's preaching.

☐ T | ☒ F   11. The king decreed that all men and animals should fast and put on sackcloth.

☒ T | ☐ F   12. God turned from destroying Nineveh because the people turned from their evil ways.

☐ T | ☒ F   13. Jonah rejoiced with the people in the salvation of the city.

☐ T | ☒ F   14. The Lord caused a gourd to grow to provide Jonah with food.

☒ T | ☐ F   15. God compared Jonah's selfish concern for the plant to His own compassion for the city.

THE BIGGEST CATCH OF ALL

Jonah preached to Nineveh, the capital of Assyria. The king of Nineveh often fought with Israel. He threatened both Israel and Judah, forcing them to pay tribute (taxes). No wonder Jonah trembled at the thought of preaching in this king's capital city. He had bad news for the enemy. They would certainly kill him.

But when the people listened to him and repented, Jonah was still unhappy. His prophecy of destruction would not come true. Jonah thought God was too soft-hearted, so he complained.

Then God taught Jonah that he was just as soft-hearted as God, only in a selfish way. He became upset over a withered plant. God questioned him, "If you can be upset over one plant, why can't I be upset over a city full of people?"

Hey, Jonah! Remember God __loves__ all __nations__, and God __forgive__ all those who __repent__. Most of the Old Testament deals with God's relationship to the nation of Israel. The book of Jonah is evidence that God has always intended to draw a people to Himself from all nations, peoples, tribes, and languages.

THINK ABOUT IT

Is your love for unbelievers more like God's or Jonah's? What evidence does your faithfulness to witness to unbelievers offer for your answer? _____

_____

_____

_____

_____

OBADIAH
NAHUM
PAYDAY FOR THE NATIONS

OBADIAH

The prophets warned Israel and Judah of the coming destruction that was the consequence of their sin. God had been patient. He kept loving them even when they turned to idols. He forgave them again and again.

But finally, God declared a payday. Israel and Judah would not get mercy on that day; they would get exactly what they had earned. The payment for sin would be destruction.

The nations around Israel also refused to obey God. After God used those nations to punish Israel and Judah, He promised to exact payment for their sin too.

Prophet to: _____ (vs. 1)

Period: _____

Historical notes:

- Probably the _____ of the prophetic writings
- Preached during the days of _____

Message: Check your _____.

CHECK YOUR ATTITUDE

Obadiah, the shortest Old Testament book, contains God's message to _____ (1:1). Who fathered this nation? (See a Bible dictionary.) _____ What was his relationship to Israel (particularly Jacob)? (Hint: See Genesis 25.) _____ _____

The Edomites had an attitude problem. In the blanks below, name the sins of which God accused them.

- _____ (vs. 3)

  What does God eventually do when men commit this sin? (See vs. 4 and James 4:6.) _____

  _____.

- _____ of their brothers (vs. 10–14)

  What does God decree about Edom's future in verses 10, 16, and 18?

  _____

  _____

NAHUM

Prophet to: _____

Period: _____ after Israel's fall

Historical note: Nahum prophesied concerning the fall of _____

Message: God is _____, but He _____ evil.

NOW IT'S YOUR TURN

Nahum predicted Nineveh's fall 130 years after Jonah's revival in that city. Nahum most likely did not travel to the city to preach there. Although his message is about Nineveh, it was meant for the ears of Judah.

Samaria, capital of the northern kingdom, fell to the king of Assyria (2 Kings 17). The king took captives back to Nineveh. He brought foreigners to live in Samaria. While Nahum preached, the new king of Assyria threatened Judah. So Nahum encouraged his fellow citizens of Judah by prophesying against the king and his capital, Nineveh.

What sins did Nineveh commit?

- 1:11: _____

  _____

- 1:14: _____

- 3:1a, 3: _____

- 3:1b: _____

How will God punish Nineveh (1:8, 14–15; 2:1–10)?

_____

_____

GOD'S PATIENCE AND GOD'S WRATH

Nahum does not prophesy simply to warn Nineveh. His words were first heard and read by citizens of Judah. God sent this message to encourage Judah. They were wondering why God let this ruthless nation take control of the world. When would God give them what they deserved?

While promising destruction for Nineveh, God promised splendor for Judah (2:2). Judah rejoiced over this prophecy (3:19) because of what it meant for them—freedom from the yoke of bondage (1:13).

Notice how Nahum introduced this prophecy of destruction. He described the wonderful God. He showed that God must punish evil (1:2–3). But he also said that God is patient. God has a long fuse before His anger is unleashed (1:3). The prophets repeat the same theme. God is just—He will judge the wicked—but He will be patient with His people.

What is the only group of people that needs to fear God's wrath (1:2)?

_____

THINK ABOUT IT

Why does God's justice require that He punish evil?

_____

_____

_____

_____

GOD IS NOT ASLEEP

MICAH

Prophet to: _____ (1:1)

Period: _____

Historical note: Micah preached during the fall of the _____ kingdom

Message: Be _____ (6:8). Put away _____. Help the _____.

GOD KNOWS YOUR SIN

Micah preached to both the northern and southern kingdoms. He predicted _____ (Israel's) destruction, which came during his lifetime (1:6). But because he lived in _____, a town south of Jerusalem, his written message concerns mostly Judah (1:1).

During Micah's time, Judah and Israel did not see any benefit in worshipping the one true God. They preferred many gods. They also felt safe in doing whatever they pleased. God did not seem to care.

But Micah warned that *God* cared. He saw what they were doing. Micah's warning was, "God is not asleep!"

Of what sins does Micah accuse Judah?

2:1: _____

2:2: _____

2:6, 11; 3:5: _____

2:9; 3:1–3: _____

3:11: _____

5:12: _____

5:13–14: _____

GOD PLANS PUNISHMENT

"These sins cannot be allowed to go on," Micah explained. "God is not asleep. He is laying plans for your punishment."

What will happen to Samaria?

1:6: _____
_____

1:7: _____

How will God punish Judah?

1:16: _____

3:12: _____

6:14: _____

6:16: _____

GOD PROMISES RESCUE

According to 4:2–3, what does God promise will happen in the last days?

_____
_____
_____

Through what group of people will God fulfill these promises (4:6–7; 5:7–8)?

R ___ ___ ___ ___ ___ ___

What does God promise in 5:2?

_____

In what New Testament verse is Micah 5:2 quoted and in the passage its fulfillment in Christ is explained? _____

HE'S STILL NOT SLEEPING

Look at the previous three major headings in this lesson. Micah's threefold outline is the message of the New Testament gospel. Use the blanks to summarize the following New Testament verses:

- God knows your sin.

  Romans 3:23: _____

- God plans punishment.

  Luke 13:5: _____

  Romans 6:23: _____

  Revelation 21:8: _____

- God promises rescue.

  Romans 6:23: _____

  Colossians 1:13–14: _____

Take Micah's advice. According to Micah 6:8, what three things does the Lord require of His people?

- _____

- _____

- _____

THINK ABOUT IT

What areas of rebellion in your own heart are you tempted to ignore because God's punishment has not dealt with you yet?

_____

_____

_____

_____

_____

HABAKKUK
THAT'S NOT FAIR

HABAKKUK

Prophet to: _____

Period: _____ after Israel's fall

Message: God is _____, and He is in _____.

Did you ever see a good person treated badly? Or a person who always tries to help other people treated meanly?

Habakkuk was a _____ (1:1) and a _____ (3:1, 19). He lived through Josiah's revival and cried when Judah returned to idols. He rejoiced when Nineveh crumbled in 612 B.C. as Nahum had predicted. Then he saw a greater nation building power. As the Babylonian Empire began to grow, Habakkuk watched his own nation sinking into violence, idol worship, and unfair treatment of good people (1:2–4; 2:18–19).

Everything seemed unfair to Habakkuk. Good people should be rewarded. Evil Babylon should be punished. Idol worshippers should be cast out of Judah. When would God do something about all of this unfairness?

A TALK WITH GOD

Complete the following analysis of Habakkuk as you read through the book:

* Habakkuk's first question (1:1–4)

  _____

  _____

- The Lord's answer (1:5–11)

  _____

  _____

- Habakkuk's second question (1:12–2:1)

  _____

  _____

- The Lord's second answer (2:2–20)

  - _____ (2:2–12)

  - _____ (2:13–20)

- Habakkuk's _____ (3:1–19)

  _____

  _____

HABAKKUK'S LESSON

Habakkuk learned that God is in control. God has a plan, and He works that plan for the benefit of His name and His people. God is faithful to His people. (See Romans 8:28.) He keeps His promises.

What should we do when everything seems to be getting out of control or when we wonder if God is ever going to do something?

> Define *faithful*:
>
>

To help you grow in your confidence in God, even through bad times, read and memorize Habakkuk 3:17–19.

THINK ABOUT IT

What circumstances tempt you to doubt God's faithfulness? How can you over-
come that temptation? _____
_____
_____
_____

Z E P H A N I A H
THE DAY OF THE LORD IS NEAR!

ZEPHANIAH

Prophet to: _____

Period: _____ after Israel's fall

Message: Prepare for God's _____ of _____.

ZEPH-WHO?

Zephaniah was a prince in the royal house of Judah. His great-great grandfather was King _____ (1:1). In this position, he could fairly denounce the sins of the _____ (1:8). He preached during the reign of _____ in Judah several years before Josiah's reform and revival.

Zephaniah claims boldly that he received this message as "the _____ of the _____" (1:1).

THE BIG MATCH

Zephaniah makes a number of promises and predictions. In the following exercise, match the prediction on the left with the proper reference on the right.

	1. Philistia will be destroyed.	A. 1:7, 14
	2. God will destroy those in Judah who worship false gods.	B. 2:1–3
	3. The day of the Lord's judgment will come soon.	C. 2:12–15
		D. 1:4–6
	4. What "that day" will be like	E. 1:10–13
	5. God will punish the wealthy.	F. 1:15–18
		G. 2:8–11
	6. Seeking the Lord is Judah's only chance for finding shelter from His anger.	H. 2:4–7
	7. God will restore Jerusalem.	I. 3:14–20
	8. Moab and Ammon will be destroyed.	
	9. Ethiopia (Cush) and Assyria will be destroyed.	

THE BIG DAY

List every verse where Zephaniah uses the word *day* to refer to the great Day of the Lord. Include references such as *that day* and *the day*. (Hint: you should find twenty such uses of *day* in thirteen verses.)

_____

_____

Now list all of the preceding references that speak of God's punishment in the left column of the following table. All references to God's blessing or help should go in the right column. Some may fit in both columns.

Day of Punishment	Day of Blessing

The day of judgment when God poured out His anger against Judah came when Nebuchadnezzar destroyed Jerusalem about fifty years after Zephaniah's prophecy. The day of blessing came seventy years later, when God began to rebuild His people with the remnant. This day of blessing also pointed toward an even greater day when God would bless the world with Christ.

As Christians, we await another great Day of the Lord. It will be a day of both punishment and blessing. Examine the following verses and list three things that we can expect on that day:

Revelation 19:15–18: _____

Revelation 19:19–20:3: _____

Revelation 20:4–6: _____

THINK ABOUT IT

If God judged his chosen people because they worshipped false gods, what can you conclude about young people in churches or Christian schools who choose to value other things more than God?

_____

_____

_____

_____

H A G G A I
Z E C H A R I A H
NEVER GIVE UP!

HAGGAI

Prophet to: _____ in _____

Period: _____

Historical note:

- Reconstruction of the _____ had stopped because of _____.

- He encourages them to _____.

Message: Make God's _____ your _____.

I QUIT!

The remnant that Zerubbabel led back to Jerusalem began rebuilding the temple with great enthusiasm. But the foreigners living in the area made fun of them. Repeatedly, they told the Jews that they would never finish. They sent bands of raiders to burn and knock down the work. Some of them wrote to the new king of Persia. They made up lies against the Jews.

Finally, the king issued an order to stop the rebuilding (Ezra 4:21, 24). The Jews felt so discouraged that they did not fight the king's order. They quit work on the temple.

For ten years, the people rebuilt their own houses. They lived comfortably while God's temple lay in ruins (Hag. 1:4). Then Haggai and Zechariah came with messages of encouragement.

- What command from God did Haggai bring (1:2, 7–8)?

  _____

- How did Zerubbabel and the people respond to God's Word (1:12; Ezra 5:1–2)?_____

- What promise did Haggai bring from God to encourage the people in their work (1:13)?_____

- How did God fulfill this promise (1:14)?

  _____

  _____

Almost two months later, the people became discouraged again. The temple looked so plain in contrast to Solomon's gorgeous temple that had been destroyed (2:1–3; Ezra 3:12). What two promises did Haggai bring from God to encourage the Jews (2:4–9)?

Verses 4–5: _____
_____.

Verses 6–9: _____
_____

ZECHARIAH

Prophet to: _____ in _____

Period: _____

Historical note: His grandfather, _____, was chief of a family of _____ who returned to _____ with _____.

Message: God will _____ His people. The _____ will come and build God's _____.

DON'T QUIT! HELP IS ON THE WAY!

Zechariah also encouraged the remnant. Whereas Haggai preached, Zechariah wrote poetry about his visions. Through these two prophets, God gave both words and pictures to His people.

With what three promises did Zechariah encourage the people?

- 1:16–17: _____
  _____

- 2:3–5: _____
  _____

- 2:10–11: _____
  _____

ZECHARIAH'S MESSIAH

Zechariah foretells truths about Christ (the Messiah) more than any other prophet but Isaiah. He encourages the remnant with the promise of God's greatest leader.

- By what two titles is Christ called in 3:8? (Compare to John 13:1–17.)

  - _____

  - _____

- Christ will enter Jerusalem on a _____, the foal of a donkey (9:9; Matt. 21:4–7).

- Christ will be _____ for thirty _____ of _____ (11:12–13; Matt. 26:14–16; 27:3–10).

- Christ will be _____ (12:10; John 19:32–37).

- Christ will cleanse from _____ and _____ (13:1; Eph. 5:26; Heb. 10:22).

- They will _____ the _____ (Christ), and the sheep will be _____ (13:7; Matt. 26:31).

These prophecies reminded the Jews that God controlled the world and that they could trust Him. What was Zechariah's message from God to Zerubbabel in 4:6 about how he would be strengthened to finish the temple?

_____

_____

_____

THINK ABOUT IT

Is God a discourager or an encourager? What hope does He offer those who submit to Him?

_____

_____

_____

_____

KEEPING PROMISES

MALACHI

Prophet to: _____ in _____

Period: _____

Historical note: Prophesied during _____ governship

Message: God is _____, so you be _____ too.

BRING YOUR BEST

Malachi prophesied to the _____ in Judah and Israel under _____ governorship. He was the _____ Old Testament prophet, completing his service about _____.

The _____ of _____ had been rebuilt. The _____ was complete. The people finished rebuilding their _____. _____ still ruled over them. But the Jews enjoyed great _____ under that rule.

Everyone became _____—in fact, too comfortable. They grew _____ in following God's _____ and in their _____. God sent _____ to stir them up.

What complaints did God bring against the Jews in the following verses?

1:6–9: _____

1:12–13: _____

2:7–8: _____

2:11–12: _____

_____

2:13–16: _____

2:17: _____

3:8–9: _____

MALACHI AND THE MESSIAH

In chapter four, Malachi predicted the _____.
It will be a day of severe _____ on all who do _____
(4:1). But it will also be a time of _____, spiritual
_____, and joy (4:2).

Malachi predicted that God would send _____ before that day (4:5).
How did Jesus say this prophecy was fulfilled (Matt. 11:10–14)? _____
_____

Who confirmed the prophecy and this interpretation to Zechariah the priest in
Luke 1:11–17? _____

THINK ABOUT IT

In what areas of your Christian walk might you be a little too comfortable?

_____

_____

_____

_____

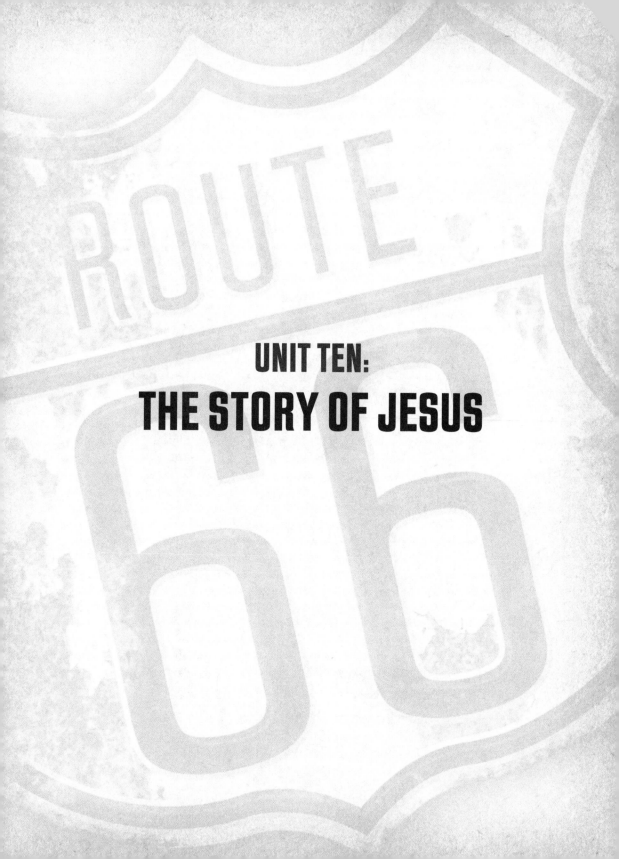

UNIT TEN:
THE STORY OF JESUS

LESSON 44
GOSPELS
GREAT NEWS

The word *gospel* means "good news." Jesus brought good news from God. He called His message of salvation "the gospel." The four books written about the life, death, and resurrection of Jesus came to be known as the Gospels. They tell how the good news came to us.

Each of the four Gospels is unique. Each book presents a different viewpoint of the gospel story. Why do you think God gave us four Gospels that tell the same story?

The Gospels comprise eighty-nine chapters. Of those chapters,

- Four cover the first thirty years of Christ's life.
- Eighty-five cover the last three years of Christ's life.
- Twenty-seven of these 85 chapters cover the last eight days of Christ's life.

The emphasis of the Gospels is clearly the death, burial, and resurrection of Christ.

THE GOSPEL ACCORDING TO MATTHEW: BEHOLD YOUR KING

Matthew wrote to the ___Jews___. He used ___93___ quotations from the ___Old testament___ to prove that ___Jes___ was the ___prom___ ___ain___. He showed the _____ that _____ fulfilled the Old Testament ___prophicy___ about the ___messiah___. Proving that Jesus came from the family of ___king Da___ was Matthew's first step in proving that Jesus was ___promise Messi___.

Matthew focused on the ___teachin___ of Jesus. He recorded more ___parable___ of the kingdom than the other Gospel writers. His account of the ___sermon on the mount___ (chapters 5–7) is more ___complet___ than Luke's account.

THE GOSPEL ACCORDING TO MARK: BEHOLD MY SERVANT

Historical evidence suggests that Mark wrote his Gospel to the _Romans_.
He probably wrote it while in _Rome_. Explaining _Jewish terms_
and customs (5:41; 7:2–4), Mark reported the _simple_
true of Jesus' life. He gave little interpretation. Each event was described
as if Mark were an _eyewitness_ or as if he got his information from
an _eyewitness_.

One of Mark's key words is the Greek word that is usually translated as
straightway or _immediately_ and it occurs
_40_ times. Brief and to the point, Mark writes with a sense of _urgency_.
According to Mark, the time for the _Jews_, _Roman_, and _Greek_
to come to _Christ_ is _now_.

What is different about where Mark begins his story and where Matthew and
Luke begin theirs? (Compare and contrast the first few chapters of each Gospel.)

_____

_____

_____

THE GOSPEL ACCORDING TO LUKE: BEHOLD THE MAN

Luke wrote his Gospel to _Theophilus_ (1:3), probably a Roman
official. _Theophilus_ became a _Christian_, and Luke
wanted him to know and understand the details of his faith (1:4). Perhaps he had
requested from Luke a formal written record of Jesus' life. Writing to this government official made Luke's Gospel a public record. It was copied and shared freely
among the Gentiles.

Luke gave a more detailed account of the _birth of Jesus_
than do the other Gospels. He repeated many events and teachings that were also
recorded by _Matthew_ and _Mark_, but God guided him to include a
lot of _only_ material too.

Jesus' words to Zacchaeus summarize the theme of the Gospel of Luke. Copy and then memorize Luke 19:10.

For the Son of Man came to seek and to save the lost

Matthew, Mark, and Luke are called the _Synoptic_ Gospels because they record Jesus' life _from a similar point of view_. (The word _synoptic_ means to see together.) The Gospel of John, however, has a unique point of view.

THE GOSPEL ACCORDING TO JOHN: BEHOLD YOUR GOD

The Synoptics emphasized Jesus' ministry in _Galilee_; whereas John emphasized His work in _Judea_ and _Perea_. Jesus' teaching in John focused on His _____ and His relationship to _the Father_. In the Synoptics, Jesus taught mainly about the _Kingdom_. Instead of Jesus' _parables_, John recorded Jesus' _symbols_ and _illustrations_ which are sometimes called His "I am's." For example, Jesus said, "_I am the Bread of life_" (John 6:35).

"_I am the light of the world_" (John 8:12).

"_I am the good shepherd_" (John 10:11).

"_I am the true vine_" (John 15:1).

Each of these analogies helps us to understand in a simple way who Jesus is. None of these statements is found in the other Gospels.

John emphasized that _miracles_ are _signs_ to prove that Jesus is _Son of God_. In all, John presented the following five different kinds of proofs:

- _apostolic testimony_
- _Jesus' own teaching_

213

- _Jesus's miracles_
- _John the Baptist's testimony_
- _Old Testament prophets_

What did John say he hoped to accomplish by writing down these proofs (20:30–31)?

_____

_____

_____

_____

THINK ABOUT IT

Why do you think God gave us four Gospels that tell much of the same story?

_____

_____

_____

GOSPELS

THE MESSIAH HAS COME

WHO IS JESUS?

Each Gospel writer introduces his readers to Jesus in the first few chapters. What does each writer say about who Jesus is?

MATTHEW

- 1:1: A descendant of Abraham and David
- 1:18–25: The Son of God and the son of Mary, whose husband was Joseph

MARK

- 1:1,11: the son of God

LUKE

- 2:11: Savior messiah
- 2:30: God salvation
- 2:32: A light for Gentiles and the glory of Isreal

JOHN

- 1:1: God
- 1:3: Creator
- 1:29: the Lamb of God
- 1:34: Chosen one

THE CHRIST IS BORN!

Using Matthew 1–2 and Luke 1–2, find the proper order of the miracles and events surrounding Jesus' birth. Number the following events from 1 to 11.

___6___ Jesus is born. Mary wraps Him in strips of cloth (swaddling clothes) and lays Him in a manger.

___11___ Mary, Joseph, and Jesus return to Nazareth after God warns Joseph in a dream to stay away from Judea.

___7___ An angel announces the birth of Jesus to shepherds.

___8___ Mary and Joseph present Jesus in the temple. Simeon blesses the baby. Anna praises God and thanks Him for Jesus.

___4___ John the Baptist is born.

___10___ Mary, Joseph, and Jesus flee to Egypt after the angel's warning.

___1___ An angel visits Zacharias (Zechariah).

___2___ The angel Gabriel tells Mary that she will have God's Son.

___9___ Wise men from the East visit Jesus after being led by the star of Bethlehem.

___5___ Mary and Joseph travel to Bethlehem because of the census (taxing).

___3___ Joseph follows the command of the angel and takes Mary as his wife.

JOHN THE BAPTIST PREPARES THE WAY

What did John preach?

- Matthew 3:1–2: _____

_____

- Luke 3:2–3: _____

_____

John fulfilled the prophecy of ___*Isaiah*___, which said that God would
___*prepared the way of Jesus*___ (Mark 1:2–4).

JESUS BEGINS HIS MINISTRY

The Bible tells us little about Jesus' childhood and early adult life. How does Luke summarize this period of time in 2:52?

_____

_____

At about the age of _*30*_ (Luke 3:23), Jesus left home to begin His ministry. What events mark the beginning of Jesus' ministry?

- Matthew 3:13–17: ___*The Baptism of Jesus*___

  Read verse 17 and tell what this event proved.
  ___*God approved of Jesus, Jesus*___
  ___*was his son*___

- Matthew 4:1–11: ___*Tempted of Jesus*___

  What did this event prove? ___*Jesus roghted to Satin*___
  ___*Knew the he word of God*___
  _____

- Luke 4:14–22: ___*teaching at the*___

  According to Matthew 4:17, what was Jesus' main message when He began to preach? ___*Repent + Leave in*___
  _____

- Mark 1:16–20: ___*the teaching of Jesus*___

Define *disciple*: *follow student*

THINK ABOUT IT

What do the names and titles of Jesus used in the early chapters of the Gospels reveal about who He is and why He came?

_____

_____

_____

_____

_____

G O S P E L S
JESUS' MINISTRY OF TEACHING

JESUS' PRONOUNCEMENTS

It is important that we understand the basic ideas that Jesus taught. Using the following Scriptures, find thirteen important ideas that Jesus taught:

- Matthew 5:43–48 _Love y__ a_
- Matthew 6:5–6 _Pray _____
- Matthew 18:21–35 _Repecertng (or disthe ce_
- Mark 2:23–28 _rest on the sabbath day_
- Mark 12:28–31 _Disciples must sacrifice ga_
- Luke 9:22 _Jesus must suffer_
- Luke 9:23–25 _Jesus f __ lovu m ost_
      geny treasur
- Luke 12:22–26 _Trust God instead of money_
- Luke 13:3 _Repent or Perish_
- Luke 19:10 _seek an sare the lost_
- John 3:1–8 _Born again_
- John 4:23–24 _Worship God_
- John 14:6 _Jesus is true_

JESUS' PARABLES

Define *parable*:

Short story w/ c a g/so,

Jesus told parables to help people picture the heavenly truths that He taught. Each parable was designed to teach one central truth. He drew His parables from real-life situations.

Not everyone understood Jesus' parables. Even the disciples asked Jesus to explain them. Some of Jesus' parables are clear in meaning to us because we have the benefit of looking back on history. Others are not so clear. What do you think might help you understand Jesus' parables better?

- look for a v Mone
- Skcinto his other cleoas
- Askeod for wisedsn

Notice that John does not record any parables. Instead, he records many illustrations and examples. What illustrations of Jesus does he relate in the following passages?

- 10:1–18: Hi is the shepsey hid is the shap
- 15:1–8: He is the vine were the Branches

JESUS' PROMISES

In His teaching, Jesus made many promises to His disciples and the people. Among other things, He promised to help them, heal them, lead them, supply their needs, forgive them of sin, and love them. Although they did not understand it, Jesus promised to die for them too. His final promise as He left earth was that He would return again.

In this section, we will look at three of the greatest promises Jesus made.

- What does Jesus promise to build in Matthew 16:18? _____

_____ *His church*

Jesus began building His church with His disciples. He had many followers. After Jesus left the earth, these men (except Judas, who had betrayed Jesus) became apostles and leaders in the church. Read Matthew 10:2–4 and then list the twelve disciples of Jesus.

1. *Simon Peter*	2. *Andrew*	3. *James*
4. *John*	5. *Philip*	6. *Barth.*
7. *Thomas*	8. *Matthew*	9. *James II*
10. *Thaddaeus*	11. *Simon zealot*	12. *Judas*

- In John 16:5–15, whom does Jesus promise to send to His disciples after He leaves? *the holy spirit*

_____

What kind of things would He do?

- John 14:16: *a advocate*

- John 16:8: *conflict the world of sin and judgment*

- John 16:13: *Guide me truth*

- John 16:14: *Glorify christ*

In Acts 2:38–39, Peter says that all believers will receive the gift of *the holy spirit*.

What is the greatest promise of Jesus (John 3:16)?
who believe him recieved eternal life

Jesus makes this promise to you too. How do you receive this promise?
trust believe accept

THINK ABOUT IT

Which of Jesus' pronouncements do you think is most important and why?

[handwritten] obeying yourself because love patience and loving kind

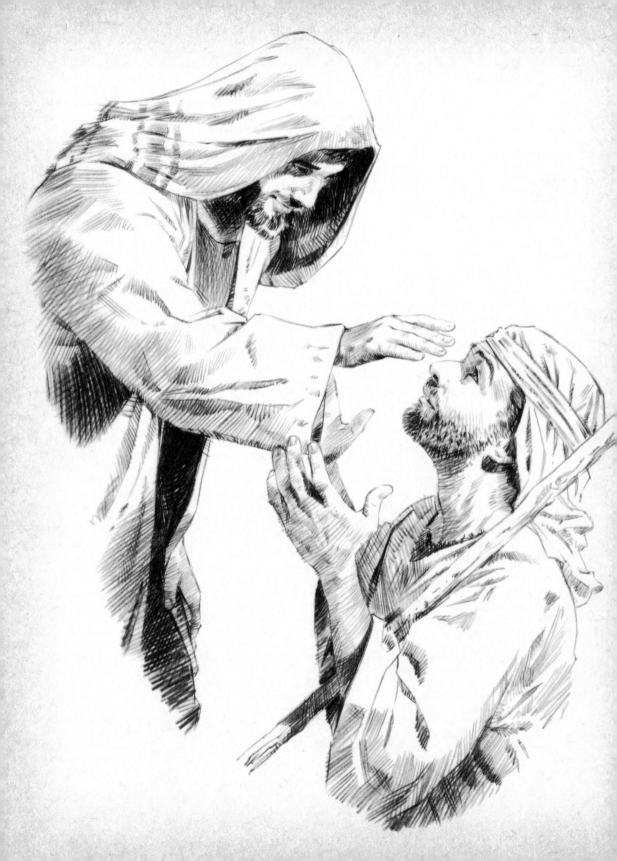

G O S P E L S

JESUS' MINISTRY OF MIRACLES

Jesus showed His love for people by helping them in ways no one else could. He healed them without medicine. He fed them by turning water into wine and a few fish into many fish. He cast evil spirits out of people, giving freedom from Satan. However, Jesus' miracles not only helped people, but they also proved that He came from God.

People whispered about Jesus, "Do you think He really is the Messiah?"

"He must be. No one could perform all of these signs and miracles if He were not from God."

Define *miracle*:

JESUS' GREAT POWER

Jesus' miracles teach us about who He is and what He can do. The following verses relate some of Jesus' miracles. Read about and identify each of these miracles. After thinking about what each group of miracles has in common, state what each group teaches us about Jesus.

- Jesus has power over _disease_.

    Matthew 9:1–8: _heal paralcaris_

    Mark 7:31–37: _heal deafishess_

    Luke 4:40: _heal many sickness_

    John 5:1–9: _heal also on an_

- Jesus has power over _____faith_____.

  Matthew 9:18–25: _____raises a dead girl_____

  Luke 7:11–15: _____raises a widow's son_____

  John 11:38–44: _____raises Lazarus_____

- Jesus has power over _____Satan_____.

  Matthew 8:28–34: _____heals two demon possessed men_____

  Mark 9:14–27: _____heals a boy with evil boy_____

  Luke 4:41: _____cast out demons_____

- Jesus has power over _____Nature_____.

  Matthew 8:23–27: _____calm a storm_____

  Luke 9:10–17: _____feeds 5000 with 5 loaves and fish_____

  John 2:1–11: _____changes water into wine_____

MIRACLE MATCH

Match each passage on the left with the correct miracle on the right.

P	1.	Matthew 8:1–4	A.	Jesus walks on water.
A	2.	Matthew 14:22–33	B.	Jesus heals ten men of leprosy.
C	3.	Matthew 15:32–39	C.	Jesus feeds four thousand.
H	4.	Mark 8:22–26	D.	Jesus cures a man with leprosy.
E	5.	Mark 9:2–8	E.	Jesus is transfigured.
G	6.	Luke 5:17–26	F.	Jesus changes water into wine.
B	7.	Luke 17:11–19	G.	Jesus heals a paralyzed man.
F	8.	John 2:1–11	H.	Jesus heals a blind man.
I	9.	John 4:15–19, 28–29	I.	Jesus knows all about a woman He has never met.

THINK ABOUT IT

What do Jesus' miracles reveal about who He is compared to all other men?

That he is the one God and is with God

4/5

G O S P E L S
JESUS DIES, BUT…

A SAVIOR WHO DIES?

How do you convince your close friends that you are about to die when they can see that you are in good health? Jesus tried to explain what would happen to Him, but His disciples did not understand. They knew that the Jewish leaders did not like Jesus and wanted to kill Him; however, they did not believe that Jesus would ever let them touch Him.

The disciples thought that Jesus, as the Messiah, would live a long and prosperous life. Expecting Him to save the Jews by His leadership, they had no idea that He would die to save them from sin. How could anyone be saved if the Savior was killed? Later, however, they understood that Jesus died to save people from a greater enemy than Rome—sin and death.

Who arrested Jesus in the garden (Luke 22:47–53)? _chef priest, guard, sewish ledders_

Who lied about knowing Jesus (Matt. 26:69–75)? _peter_

Who was the Roman governor who tried Jesus (Matt. 27:11–14)? _Pilte_

What things happened immediately after Jesus' death (Matt. 27:50–54; Luke 23:44–48)?

_____

_____

Who buried Jesus? Where (Matt. 27:57–60)? _____

_____

THE MISSING BODY

What did the women discover at the tomb (Matt. 28:1–7)?

the stone was rolled away
angel told them jesus had risen

One of the first people to whom Jesus appeared after He rose from the dead was _Mary Magdic_ (John 20:10–18).

How did the disciples know for sure that Jesus was alive (John 20:19–20)?

They saw Him.

How did Thomas know that He was alive (John 20:24–29)?

He saw Him and touched His wounds.

Who else saw Jesus after He arose (Luke 24:13–35)?

two disciples on the road

Jesus' death meant little if He remained dead, but His resurrection proved that His power was greater than death.

Jesus died to provide forgiveness for our sins. He arose to give us life. He now lives forever and is able to give us that same kind of life. Only a God who conquered death could give life that lasts forever.

- Because Jesus died on the cross, I can _be forgiven_.
- Because Jesus rose from the dead, I can _live forever_.

I'LL BE RIGHT BACK!

Jesus appeared on earth for forty days after His resurrection. Then He returned to heaven. Now He has taken His heavenly throne. He has accomplished His mission.

What commands did Jesus give before leaving His disciples?

- Matthew 28:18–20: _make disciples throught the word_
- Acts 1:8: _be His witness_

What promises did Jesus make before leaving His disciples?

- Matthew 28:20: _He is always with us_
- Luke 24:49; Acts 1:8: _Give us power of the holyspirit_

What promise did the angels make the disciples after Jesus ascended into heaven?

- Acts 1:10–11: _Jesus will return_.

While Jesus is away, He wants me to…

Make disciples, forthing shar. His good new

THINK ABOUT IT

If you were to become more obedient to Jesus' command to make disciples throughout the world, what would have to change in your life?

_____

_____

_____

_____

_____

_____

UNIT ELEVEN:
BUILDING ON CHRIST'S FOUNDATION

LESSON 49

ACTS

THE BIRTH OF THE CHURCH

Acts is the only book in the history division of the New Testament. The Gospels record a special portion of history, but Acts is a formal history of the birth of the church.

OVERVIEW OF ACTS

Compare Acts 1:1–5 with Luke 1:1–4; 24:48–49 to answer the following questions:

- Who wrote the book of Acts? _Luke_

- To whom is Acts written? _Theophilue_

- At what point in history does Acts begin? _?esus Ascends_ _to heaven_

To set the stage, Acts tells how Jesus gave final instructions to His disciples and left them. Jesus did not stay around to begin the church Himself. He left it in the hands of His disciples, who would lead the church by the power of the Spirit.

What instructions did Jesus give His disciples about what they were to do after He left (Acts 1:4)? _wait in jerusalem_ _for the holy spirit_

What promises did Jesus give them (Acts 1:5–8)?

- _The would be baptized with holy spirit_
- _they would be His witnesses to the Holy spirit_

In Acts 1:8, Jesus predicted a three-stage plan for spreading His good news. What was it? They were to be His _witnesses_ in…

1. _Jerusalem_
2. _Judea_ and _Samaria_
3. _the uttermost part of the earth_

We will see this plan in action as we study the book of Acts.

CHOOSING ANOTHER APOSTLE

After betraying Jesus, Judas took his own life. The disciples decided that they should fill his position with someone else. But how would they decide who should be the twelfth apostle? First, they decided on two basic requirements. According to Acts 1:21–22, what were those qualifications?

1. _to have been with Jesus - to have been with Jesus_

2. _seen Jesus after resurrection_

From among those who fulfilled these requirements, they chose two men. Then they prayed and cast lots (much like drawing straws) to make the final selection. Who was chosen (Acts 1:23–26)? _Matthus_

> Define *apostle:* _a sent one_

As Acts begins, Jesus' disciples are no longer followers. Their leader had left, and now they had become the leaders. They are no longer called disciples but apostles. Instead of following, they are sent out to preach, teach, and lead.

THE DAY OF PENTECOST

The Feast of _Pentacost (a. week)_ came fifty days after the Sabbath of _Passover_. Jesus died and rose on Passover weekend, and the events of Acts 2 occurred on Pentecost, about fifty days later. Jesus appeared to His disciples for _to_ days after He arose (Acts 1:3).

That means that the apostles waited for the promised Holy Spirit for about _10_ days after Jesus ascended.

List the three miracles that occurred on the Day of Pentecost (Acts 2).

2:2: _a sound like blowing of a mighty wind_

2:3: _tongues of fire resting upon them_

2:4: _the apostles speaking in other languages._

- How did the people respond to these miracles (2:5–12)? _They were amazed, were perplexed, and amused within hearts_

- Peter claimed that God was fulfilling a promise made through the prophet _Joel_ (2:16). In your own words, write the first part of the prophecy quoted by Peter (2:17a). _God will reach us and give us all vision_

- What did Peter declare about Jesus in 2:36? _God made Jesus_

Amazed by the miracles and the strange events of the previous few months, many people in the crowd believed Peter's message. They realized that Jesus was the promised Messiah. Afraid that God would punish them for killing Jesus, they asked Peter, "What shall we do?"

- What two things did Peter say they must do (2:38)?

  1. _repent_

  2. _be baptized_

- What two things did Peter promise those who would follow his advice (2:38)?

  1. _____ forgiveness of sin _____
  2. _____ gift of holy spirit _____

- How did the people respond (2:41)?
  _____ 3000 people believe _____

So, Christ's church began. With more than three thousand "charter members," they started a movement that would sweep through Jerusalem and Judea—and eventually the world.

WORSHIP IN THE FIRST CHURCH

We immediately see in the history of the church that four ingredients were involved in their worship. Luke writes in Acts 2:42 that the first Christians devoted themselves to:

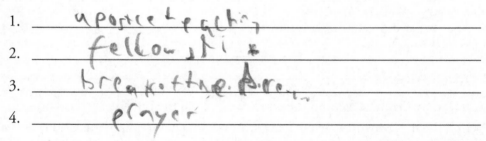

1. _____ apostle teaching _____
2. _____ fellowship _____
3. _____ break the bread _____
4. _____ prayer _____

The believers also worshipped by helping one another. They took care of one another's needs. What did they do in 2:44–45?

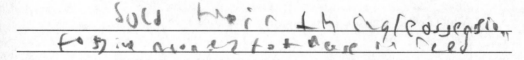

_____ Sold their th agleossepsio _____
_____ to give money to those in need _____

THINK ABOUT IT

If you had been alive to see the miracles, the preaching, and the many conversions at the Day of Pentecost, what would have surprised you most?

_____

_____

_____

_____

_____

_____

A C T S

THE CHURCH GROWS AND GROWS

PETER TAKES A STAND

After the Day of Pentecost, Peter became a strong leader among believers. The Holy Spirit made him bold. No longer did he feel ashamed to say that he followed Jesus. The first twelve chapters of Acts tell more about Peter than about any of the other apostles. He played an important role in the birth and growth of Christ's church.

After reading the following passages, tell how Peter stood up for his faith:

Acts	Peter's Courage
4:1–20	Peter & John were captured, Peter preached to jewish leader even though he was warned not to
5:1–11	confroted Ananias & saphira about their lie & helped restore the church open ly
5:12–16	healed people in public
5:17–32	Peter & the apostles kept preaching even after being arrested

OTHER BELIEVERS TAKE A STAND

Who was Stephen (Acts 6:5, 8–10)?

men full of faith and the holy spirit

What happened to Stephen when he took a stand (6:11–14; 7:54–60)?

they stoned him

Before the time of Stephen's death, the believers stayed in Jerusalem. They shared the good news with only other Jews. What happened to make the disciples scatter to other cities (Acts 8:1)?

a great persecution

How did the Holy Spirit use this persecution to fulfill Jesus' words about their being witnesses for Him in Jerusalem, Judea, and Samaria? Give a specific example (8:4–8).

Philip went to Samaria

Philip met an ___Ethiopian eunuch___ on a desert road (8:26–28). The man was reading from ___Isaiah___ about ___Jesus___ ___in his death___ (8:30–33). Philip taught him ___about the good news___ (8:35).

When he heard this message from Philip, the ___eunuch___ wanted to ___be baptized___ (8:36–38). Philip agreed. After this, the Spirit took Philip away, and the man ___went rejoicing___ (8:39).

Since the Ethiopian went back to his African country, how did this event begin to fulfill the rest of Jesus' prophecy that the disciples would be witnesses for Him throughout the world?

Ethiopia spread a little

TO EVERY NATION

The gospel of Jesus Christ went out to many cities as the disciples traveled. But still they preached only to the Jews. No Gentiles became Christians, until one day…

246

A Roman centurion named *Cornelius* lived in *Caesarea* (10:1). He and his family were *devout* and *God-fearing*, which they proved by giving generously to *the poor* and by *praying* regularly (10:2). An *angel* told *Cornelius* to send for *Peter* in *Joppa* (10:3–5).

Before the men arrived from Cornelius, Peter saw a vision of *a sheet containing many animals* (10:9–13). Peter refused to eat the meat of these animals because he had never before eaten anything *unclean* (10:14). This meant that he had obeyed the Old Testament Law, which forbade eating certain kinds of meat. The forbidden meats were called unclean. God told him that Peter was not to call *impure* what God had *cleansed* (10:15).

God used this vision to prepare Peter to be the first apostle to take the gospel to the Gentiles. It was against the Jewish law for Jews to *associate with the Gentiles* (10:28). Jews believed that Gentiles were *unclean* (10:28). Peter realized that God was using the vision to tell him that *he should not call common or unclean any man* (10:28). So Peter went to see *Cornelius* at *Caesarea*. But he had no idea that God wanted him to do something more than just associate with Gentiles (10:29).

Cornelius explained that an angel had told him to send for Peter. He gathered his family and asked Peter to tell them *everything the Lord commanded him* (10:33). Peter told them *the good news* (10:34–43). As Peter preached, the Holy Spirit *came on / fell on those who* (10:44).

Peter and his Jewish friends were *astonished* that the gift of the Holy Spirit had been poured out on the *Gentiles* (10:45). Peter decided that these people should *be baptized* (10:47–48).

After Peter reported these events to the other apostles and believers in Jerusalem, they concluded that _God want to save the gentiles_ (11:18).

THINK ABOUT IT

What does the amazing growth of the early church reveal about God's power and His plan to build His church?

_____

_____

_____

_____

ACTS

FROM CHRISTIAN-HATER TO CHRISTIAN-MAKER

WHO WAS PAUL?

Original Hebrew name: _Saul_ (Acts 8:1; 9:1)

Changed to Greek name: _Paul_ (Acts 13:9)

Birthplace: _Tarsus_ (Acts 9:11)

Race: _Jew_ (Phil. 3:5)

Tribe: _Benjamin_ (Phil. 3:5)

Occupation: _Tent-Maker_ (Acts 18:3)

Religious group: _Pharisee_ (Phil. 3:5)

Passion: _Persecuting christians_ (Acts 9:1)

SAUL'S SUDDEN CHANGE

Read Acts 9:1–22, and put the following events in the right order by numbering them 1–10:

5	Saul discovers he is blind.	4	Jesus asks Paul why he is persecuting Him.
2	Saul's sets out for Damascus.	6	God sends Ananias to Saul.
8	Saul's blindness is healed.	7	God says that Saul will carry the gospel to Gentiles.
1	Saul persecutes the church.	9	Saul is baptized.
3	Saul sees a light and hears a voice.	10	Saul testifies for Jesus.

SAUL BECOMES PAUL

Saul changed his Jewish name to the Greek name "Paul." He wanted to reach the Romans and Greeks with the gospel. God appointed him as the apostle to the Gentiles. Essentially everyone in the Roman Empire spoke Greek. Gentiles would be more open to listen to him if he had a Greek name.

The church at _Antioch_ sent out _Paul_ and _Barnabas_ as missionaries (13:1–5).

How did people respond to their preaching?

- 13:12: _Believed_
- 13:42–43: _wanted to hear more_
- 13:48: _were glad, honored the Word_
- 14:1–7: _many believer, but some wanted to stone_

On Paul's second missionary journey, he took _Silas_ and _Timothy_ with him (15:36–16:3). While visiting the churches that he had started, Paul had a vision about _man from Macedonia needing help_ (16:9–10).

In the Macedonian city of Philippi, many families came to the Lord. Luke mentions two families among the converts. They are _Lydia_'s family and _Shipjailor_'s family (16:13–15, 25–34).

Look up the following events from Acts chapters 17–26 and match them with the names of the correct people or places:

B	1.	Paul explains the "unknown god."	A.	Apollos
D	2.	Paul meets Aquila and Priscilla.	B.	Athens
A	3.	Preacher whom Aquila and Priscilla helped understand the gospel better	C.	Caesar
E	4.	Man whom Paul raises from the dead	D.	Corinth
	5.	Said that Paul's testimony almost persuaded him to become a Christian	E.	Eutychus
F			F.	Felix
C	7.	Ruler to whom Paul appealed his case	G.	Paul
H	8.	City to which Paul and other prisoners were sent	H.	Rome
G	9.	Lived under house arrest for two years		

A PEOPLE WITH A MISSION

Jesus sent out the apostles to preach and teach His Word. The church sends out missionaries to preach and teach Christ's Word today. Just as the church at Antioch sent out Paul and others, churches today send missionaries all over the world.

- Six missionary principles:

   1. Missionaries were ___sent out by the___ ___church___ (Acts 13:1–4).

   2. Missionaries went to ___synagogues, places___ ___meeting___ (13:5, 14; 17:17–23).

   3. Missionaries preached to everyone, but _____ (13:44–51).

   4. Missionaries worked hard at _____ (18:4).

5. A missionary not only started churches but also _came back_
to visit and encourage strengthen
them (14:21–23).

6. Some missionaries supported themselves by _with_
other jobs (18:1–4).

THINK ABOUT IT

Why would God miraculously save a person whose passion in life was to persecute Christians? _So God shows he has power over_
evil

UNIT TWELVE:
PAUL'S LETTERS

ROMANS
HOORAY FOR THE GOSPEL!

WHAT'S IT ALL ABOUT?

Romans is a letter…

- from _____, who described himself as a servant of _____ _____ (1:1).

- to all who are in _____, _____ of God (1:7).

GOD'S GREAT GOSPEL

- Why does Paul say he is not ashamed of the gospel of Jesus Christ (1:16)?
  _____
  _____

- According to Romans 1:19–20, God revealed truth about Himself to all men before Jesus came. How did God do this? _____

- Instead of accepting God's plain revelation of Himself, men:

  - Exchanged _____ for _____ _____ (1:23).

  - Exchanged the _____ for a _____ and served created things rather than the _____ (1:25).

  - Exchanged _____ for _____ , meaning they _____(1:26–27).

  - Became filled with _____ (1:29).

JESUS MAKES US RIGHT WITH GOD

Define *justify*:

OUR NEED

We all need to be made right with God because we have _____
and _____
(Rom. 3:23).

Sin separates us from God. It is disobedience.

GOD'S ANSWER

To bring us back to Himself, God presented Jesus as a _____
(3:25), meaning that Jesus paid the price for our sin. We do not get the punishment we deserve. Jesus takes our punishment while we go free!

This is how Jesus makes us right with God. He forgives our sin through His blood on the cross. Then we can come to God.

We have been _____ through _____ (5:1). We have
_____ with _____ through _____ _____ (5:1).

GOD'S LOVE

At just the right time, when we were without _____, Christ died for
_____ (5:6). But God shows His own _____ for us in
this: _____ (5:8).

THE GOSPEL OF FREEDOM

According to Romans 6:3–5, how is a believer united with Jesus Christ in His death, burial, and resurrection?

_____

_____

Being dead to sin means:

- _____
  _____ (6:12).

- _____
  _____ (6:13).

- _____ (6:14).

Being alive to God means:

- _____ (6:13).

- _____
  _____ (6:13).

- _____
  _____ (6:18).

Paul summarizes this section in 6:23 by saying that the _____ of sin is _____. Before Adam and Eve sinned, death did not exist in God's creation. The payment for Adam's sin was death. The payment for our own sin is spiritual death—that is, separation from God.

God's gift is _____ (6:23). That gift cannot be earned. It is free. God gives it to us. Death is earned, but life is a free gift.

GOD'S SOVEREIGNTY IN THE GOSPEL

Romans chapters 9–11 reveal four important truths about how He has offered salvation to different groups of people.

- God planned for His own purposes a special _____
  for Himself with _____ and His _____,
  the Israelites.

- Israel failed to keep their part in that relationship, or _____,
  because they did not pursue it by _____.

- God now makes salvation and a special relationship with Him available to
  all _____—to any who will _____.

- God will still save any _____ who live by _____, not
  _____.

HOW TO LIVE BY THE GOSPEL

- According to Romans 12:1, how are we to worship and serve God?
  _____
  _____

- What does Paul mean when he says, "be transformed" (12:2)?
  _____

- How is a Christian to behave toward the government (13:1–7)?
  _____

- What one debt do all Christians always have (13:8)?
  _____

- What is the strong Christian to do for weak Christians (15:1–2)?
  _____

Define *edify*:

Paul points out one important duty that every Christian has—to edify, or build
up, other Christians.

Christians meet together because they need encouragement from people who have the same faith. They also meet because they have a responsibility to help others. Christianity is not something that a person can do or have alone. It is a group activity. Each member cares for and helps another. Some people believe they can serve God on their own and that they do not need the church. Unfortunately, this attitude denies what Scripture teaches about our dependence on others in the body of Christ. God did not create us to worship and serve Him on our own.

THINK ABOUT IT

How can you help other Christians to worship and serve God?

_____

_____

_____

What is the gospel?

_____

_____

_____

_____

I   C O R I N T H I A N S
ONE BODY

WHAT'S IT ALL ABOUT?

First Corinthians is a letter…

- from _Paul_ and _Sosthenes_ (1:1) while they were in _Ephesus_ (16:8).

- to _to the church of Corinth_ (1:2).

Had Paul written to Corinth before (1 Cor. 5:9)? _Yes_

How did Paul hear from them before this letter (1:11; 16:17)?

othrrded reporter might as
salizay

Paul wrote to the Corinthians for several reasons. Identify them in the following verses:

1:11–13: _Division of the church_

2:1–5; 15:1: _Ripory from ot God power_

3:1–3: _Ihnyar true actly wudly_

4:18–19: _They wer arrose_

5:1–2: _Immoftis colarian sin_

7:1; 8:1; 12:1: _Ninswer their question_

11:21–22: _Misurtntikne lord supper_

UNITY IN GOD'S SPIRIT

The theme of Paul's first letter to Corinth is unity. He felt upset when he heard about all the divisions among them. These divisions caused many problems. Paul shows them that their problems can be solved by the unity of God's Spirit. In Christ Jesus they can become one body—one church.

We can follow Paul's advice to build unity within our church and between churches. What does he tell us we can do in the following passages?

3:1–9: _Follow Christ, not man_

5:1–5, 11–13: _Do not associate with immorality_ _____

8:9–13: _Help the weak(?)_

10:31–33: _Work on pleasing others(?)_

12:4–6, 12–13: _Cooperation(?)_

12:14–21, 25–26: _Have concern for others(?)_

13:4–7: _Love others_

14:29–33, 40: _Be orderly in worship_

THINK ABOUT IT

Is unity in the church only the responsibility of adults? How can you as a young person promote unity in your church?

_____

_____

_____

_____

2   C O R I N T H I A N S
JOY IN MINISTRY

WHAT'S IT ALL ABOUT?

Second Corinthians is a letter…

- from ___Paul___ and ___timoth___ (1:1) while they were in Macedonia (2:13; 7:5).
- to ___the church of God in corinth___ and all the saints throughout ___Achai___ (1:1).

Paul writes because he plans to ___visit a ministry___ (13:1). He also wanted to explain why he did not come earlier (1:15–24). Most of all, Paul writes to defend himself.

False teachers in Corinth mocked his letter. They claimed that he was not a true apostle; therefore, his teaching did not matter. In his letter, Paul proves that he has authority to teach as an apostle of Christ.

How does Paul prove this in the following passages?

1:12: ___misconduct is holy___

3:1–3: ___the history of good things rise___

6:11–13: ___opened my heart to them___

7:2: ___wrong none___

11:7: ___free took no money___

11:23–29: ___He suffered for his teaching___

12:12: ___He performs signs or miracles___.

JOY IN SERVING JESUS

Paul said many good things about the Corinthians in his letter. His earlier letters had helped them, and they had improved. Paul showed his happiness about this improvement. For what good thing did Paul compliment the Corinthians in 1:11?

For there praying

Paul also showed joy over the service that he offers to Christ. In spite of all of the trouble he faced, Paul served Christ with joy. According to 4:16–18, what encouraged Paul when times were tough?

eternal glory

Paul summarized his ministry in 5:11, 18–20. What was the focus of his ministry according to these verses?

to preach reconsiliation

Define *reconcile*:	_Bring back togther restore_

JOY IN GENEROSITY

One of the reasons Paul wrote both 1 and 2 Corinthians was to ask their help in raising a special offering. Christians in Jerusalem needed help during a famine. Paul planned to take to Jerusalem money donated by the Christians of Macedonia, Asia, and Achaia.

What are some principles from 2 Corinthians that instruct believers about giving to God's church or providing what others need?

- _even christian giving bring joy_ (8:2).
- _exel in the grace of giving_ (8:7).
- _remeber Jesus grace_ (8:9).

- _sharing equally_ (8:13–15).
- _what he give is what jesus put on your heart_ (9:7a).
- _you are a cheerful giver_ (9:7b).
- _god da replisrn needs_ (9:11).
- _giving ceres tine raiseto God_ (9:12–13).

What are some things you can give to God that will help His church or help provide what others need?

money	good goodness
food	
time	
cloth	
equipment	

THINK ABOUT IT

What is the most basic reason for a Christian to be joyful?

that God loves you

GALATIANS

GET IT RIGHT

WHAT'S IT ALL ABOUT?

Galatians is a letter…

- from _____paul_____ an apostle sent by ___Jesus christ___ and _____God the father_____ (1:1).

- to _the church of Galatia,_ (1:2).

The apostle writes to them because __are believeing__ ___different Gospel___ _____ (1:6–7).

Paul wanted the Galatians to know that:

- His gospel came by ___Jesus christ___ (1:11–12).

- We are justified by _faith of j_ (2:16).

- Those who believe are the spiritual descendants of ___Abrah___ (3:7).

- We are all _one_ in Christ Jesus (3:28).

- We are _free_ in Christ (5:1).

HOW TO BE RIGHT WITH GOD

Some false teachers came to Galatia. They taught that the Gentiles must become Jews in order to be Christians. These teachers also insisted that Christians obey the Old Testament laws and demanded that Gentiles be circumcised and observe the Jewish holy days.

Paul says that these men preached a gospel of works. They taught that people could be saved by obeying the Law.

> Define *Gentiles*: Not jewish people

According to the following verses in Galatians, how are people justified or made right with God?

- 2:16: Faith in christ
- 3:13: through christ, redeemed us from the curse
- 3:26–27: being baptized in christ

According to the following verses, what is more important than obeying the Old Testament law?

- 5:6: Faith working through love
- 5:14: Love your neighbore as yourself
- 6:15: becoming a new creation

YIELDING TO GOD'S SPIRIT

Christians are free from sin and the Law. We are not free, however, to do as we choose without facing consequences. We are free to do right—not free to break God's law. If we obey, we are using our freedom wisely.

To use our freedom wisely, we must yield to God's Spirit. What advice does Paul give for obeying the Holy Spirit?

- 5:13: serve one humbly in love

- 5:16: _Wolk by the spirit instead of flesh_
- 6:1–2: _carry each others barden_
- 6:9–10: _So good to all people_

How can you tell if others are led by the Spirit? When people are led by the Spirit, they produce good things, just like a hard-working tree produces good fruit. Paul describes the fruit that the Spirit produces in our lives. Read Galatians 5:22–23 and then write the nine characteristics of the fruit of the Spirit in the following spaces:

Love	Joy	Peac.
Forbearance	kindess	goodness
gentleness	faithfulnes	self-control

THINK ABOUT IT

What parts of the fruit of the Spirit are most clearly present in your life? Which are most clearly absent?

the present is joy

the most absent is gentleness

E P H E S I A N S
WHAT A CHURCH!

WHAT'S IT ALL ABOUT?

Ephesians is a letter...

- from __Paul__, an apostle of __Christ Jesus__ by the will of __God__ (1:1).

- to the __saint__, at __Eph sus__ who are the __faithful__ in Christ Jesus (1:1).

While Paul wrote to scold the Corinthians and the Galatians, he wrote to praise and encourage the Ephesians. Using the following verses, find Paul's reasons for writing:

- To exalt the name of God for His overwhelmingly gracious _____ __spiritual blessing__ (1:3–14)

- To praise them for __their faith and love__ (1:15)

- To remind them that Christ __brought them near to the God__ (2:12–13)

- To urge them to live __a life worthy of their calling__ (4:1)

- To urge them to keep __the unit e ox th Sprin__ (4:3)

- To urge them to __follow God walk in love__ (5:1–2)

- To urge them to __Destroy in the Lor__ (6:10)

ALL THE DIFFERENCE IN THE WORLD

Paul tells the Ephesians that Jesus Christ makes a big difference in our lives. He says that being apart from God and full of sin is like being dead (2:1). But being forgiven by Christ is like being _____ child con deatntility, (2:5–6). Dead or alive—that's quite a difference!

The apostle also equates the difference between non-Christians and Christians to that between aliens and citizens (2:11–13). Before believing in Christ, the Ephesians were aliens or foreigners to God's covenant. When they became Christians, however, God made them citizens of His kingdom.

- *Why* did God bring us near to Himself?

  2:4: _His great love and mercy_

- *How* did God save us from sin and bring us near to Himself?

  2:8: _by grace through faith_

  2:13: _blood_

- What did God save us to *do*?

  2:10: _God works_

  2:21: _become a holy temple in the Lord_

  2:22: _become a dwelling of the spirit_

BE ONE BODY

Christians are united by Christ. Paul urges the Ephesians to maintain their unity in Christ. What seven reasons does Paul give for unity in the church?

1. There is one body.	5. There is one faith
2. There is one spirit	6. There is one baptism
3. There is one hope	7. There is one God and father
4. There is one Lord	

LIVE IN THE LIGHT

Paul uses the images of light and darkness to contrast good and evil. As Christians, we were once in _darked_, but now we are _bright_ _____ (5:8). That means that we are to live as _children_ _of light_ (5:8).

- When a wife lives in the light, she _sub int toward_ _respect her husband_ (5:22, 33).

- When a husband lives in the light, he _loves his wife_, _____ (5:25, 33).

FIGHT THE RIGHT FIGHT

Our real enemy is not _flesh and blood_ (6:12).

Our real enemy is _powers, rulers of darkness_ _spiritual wickness_ _____ (6:12).

Paul tells us to put on the armor of God so that when the devil tries to hurt us, we will _stand_ (6:13). We must fight this spiritual enemy with spiritual armor and weapons. List the pieces of spiritual armor mentioned in Ephesians 6:14–17.

- _belt of truth_
- _breastplate of righteousness_
- _gospel of peace_
- _shield of faith_
- _helmet of salvation_
- _word of God_

THINK ABOUT IT

Read Ephesians 1:3–14 again and make a list of spiritual blessings for which you can give thanks to God in your own life. Take just a couple minutes right now to express your thanks to God for these blessings.

God I'm thankful for everything
for being a good protector and being a skillful

PHILIPPIANS
REJOICE

WHAT'S IT ALL ABOUT?

Philippians is a letter…

- from _Paul_ and _Timothy_ servants of _Christ Jesus_ (1:1).

- to the _saints_ in Christ Jesus at _Philippi_ together with the _overseers_ and _deacons_ (1:1).

Paul wrote to the Philippians from _prison_ in Rome (1:13–14). He sent this letter with Tychicus, who also carried letters to Ephesus and Colosse (Eph. 6:21–22).

How did Paul feel about the Philippians?

1:3–8: _Paul felt a christ together desire in God._

4:1: _that they were a joy._

JOY IN JESUS

Although Paul wrote this letter from prison, he referred to his joy despite his circumstances. Being a servant of Jesus brings joy to our lives no matter where we are or what bad things happen to us. Unlike mere happiness, true joy doesn't decline with deteriorating or trying circumstances.

Complete the following statements about joy found in Philippians:

1:4: Paul always _pray_ with _joy_.

1:18: Paul rejoiced because _christ is preached_.

2:2: The Philippians could make Paul's joy _____complete_____ by _____like minded____
_____.

3:1: Rejoice in _____the Lord_____.

4:4: Paul repeated the command to _____rejoice_____ in the Lord.

4:10: Paul rejoiced in the Lord greatly that the Philippian believers' _____
_____cared for him_____.

What are three things that you do to develop a joyful attitude and rejoice in any situation?

- _____God is with you_____
- _____remember the Lord promises_____
- _____

BECOMING LIKE JESUS CHRIST

Paul urges the Philippians to imitate Jesus. In chapter two, Paul tells the Philippians (and us) to be humble like Jesus was. According to the following verses, in what ways did Jesus show His humility?

- 2:7: _____be a ming like a servant_____
- 2:8: _____obeyed all the Father trust of Jesus_____

In what ways can we show humility?

- 2:3: _____Don't be selfish put others first_____
- 2:4: _____think about the interest of others_____

282

Paul's goal in life was to ___Know Christ and be like him___ (3:8, 10).

What do we need to do to reach that goal (3:13–14)?
___Forget about the past Press toward the end___

THINK ABOUT IT

What direction are you headed? Are you becoming more like Christ or just making yourself happy? Think of something in your life that you need to change to become more like Christ. Write it in the space provided.

___become a Christians___

Now, how are you going to go about changing that? Come up with several ideas for how you can start today.

___have fun___

C O L O S S I A N S
GET IT STRAIGHT

WHAT'S IT ALL ABOUT?

Colossians is a letter…

- from _Paul_, an apostle of _Christ Jesus_ by the will of _God_, and from _Timothy_, a fellow Christian (Col. 1:1).
- to the _Holy_ and _faithful_ brothers in Christ at _____ (1:2).

As far as we know, Paul never went to Colosse, but he heard about their faith and love from a man named _Epaphras_ (1:7–8). _Epaphras_ took the gospel to Colosse and started a church there (1:7).

This man came to Paul at Rome and told him about the good faith and love of the Colossians. He also reported on the false teaching in Colosse. Paul wrote to these Christians from _jail_ in Rome (4:18). He encouraged them to keep loving each other and trusting in God. He also corrected the false teaching.

Paul sent the letter with _Tychicus_ (4:7), who also carried letters to Ephesus, _Laodicea_ (4:16), and to a man named Philemon, who lived in Colosse.

Colosse lay in a quiet valley with two other cities, Laodicea and Hierapolis. No major road passed through this valley, which is probably why Paul never journeyed there. But Epaphras probably met Paul at Ephesus and took the gospel back to his valley. He probably planted the churches in Laodicea and Hierapolis as well (4:12–15).

CONGRATULATIONS!

How do you feel when someone praises or compliments you? It encourages you and gives you confidence, right? Paul praised the Colossian Christians for the good things he had heard about them. He wanted them to realize that the gospel of Christ was working to change them to become more like Christ.

We do not always feel terrific about our Christian lives. Sometimes we feel as though we're failing so badly that we want to give up. We need to be reminded that we can change and become more like Christ with God's help. We can encourage others by thanking them for the great things they have done or are doing for the Lord. We should not give insincere praise, but we should seek to encourage one another to serve the Lord well and faithfully.

For what does Paul congratulate the Colossians?

- Congratulations on their ___Faith and love___ (1:3–4).
- Congratulations for ___receving the gospel___ (1:6).
- Congratulations on their ___inheritance___ (1:12).
- Congratulations on their ___free from dark___ (1:13).

The whole letter of Colossians encourages Christians to keep on serving God with the love and enthusiasm they have had. Chapter 4 lists many of Paul's friends and fellow workers whom he encourages with a brief note.

Think about what you can do to encourage other Christians. Think of someone specific and write a few sentences about how you plan to encourage that person today or this week.

___(cal:b) I plan to make caleb happy cheering with him n/ tellin meaning less joke___

THINK ETERNITY!

Paul reminds the Colossians who their Lord is. Note what he says about Jesus in each of the following verses:

1:15a: _The image of the invisible God_

1:15b: _The first born over all creation_

1:16: _He created all things_

1:17: _all things held together_

1:18: _head of the church_

1:20: _reconcile all things_

Remembering who Christ is helps us remember who we are. We are not simply people trying to survive and be happy in this world. We are forgiven sinners whom Jesus has brought near to God (1:21–22). We belong to Jesus, not ourselves. We live by trusting and obeying Him, not by doing as we please.

The Colossians forgot that they were free in Christ. They listened to false teachers, who demanded that they follow certain Old Testament laws. Those teachers insisted that the Colossians be circumcised and observe Jewish feast days. But Paul reminded the Colossians of their freedom.

Laws are temporary, but freedom in Christ will last forever. Paul urges us to focus on our forever freedom instead of the things that look good but are temporary. He tells us "Think eternity!"

According to Colossians 3:1–17, how do we "think eternity"?

3:1: _seek that eternally_

3:2: _fix desires on things above_

3:5: _put to death sinful desires_

3:12: _love is eternal_

3:17: _do everything in the name of Christ_

THINK ABOUT IT

What kinds of things do you fix your thoughts on that are incompatible with a mind and heart that is fixed on God?

_____

_____

_____

_____

_____

1 & 2 T H E S S A L O N I A N S
WAY TO GO!

WHAT'S IT ALL ABOUT?

1 & 2 Thessalonians are two letters…

- from _Paul_, _Silas_ and _Tim_ while they were at Corinth (1 Thess. 1:1; 2 Thess. 1:1).

- to _Macedonia, Thessaloni_ _____ (1:1).

Paul wrote 1 Thessalonians to commend the Christians at _Thessalon_ (Acts 17:1). He felt proud of them because (1) they became followers of the apostles ("us") and the _Lord Jesus_ and, (2) in spite of their suffering, they _the word with joy_ (1 Thess. 1:6). They became models to _all the believers_ _in Macedonia and Achaia_ (1:7). Paul also commended their faith, which had _become known to every_ (1:8).

Paul also wrote to answer questions about Christ's second coming. Some Thessalonians were confused about what will happen to Christians who die before Christ returns. In chapters 4 and 5, Paul calms their fears about the future.

Later, Paul wrote 2 Thessalonians to resolve new problems. Further confusion about the Second Coming had stirred great debate (chapter 2). Paul praised them and thanked them because their _faith_ was growing, and their _love_ was increasing (2 Thess. 1:3). They needed encouragement because _they were suffering persecution_ (2 Thess. 1:4–7).

HE'S COMING! ARE YOU GOING?

Jesus Christ is coming again. The Thessalonians did not doubt this fact, but they were confused over what would happen when He came. Someone had taught them that those who are alive at Christ's coming will have an advantage over those who have died.

Paul, however, showed that this was not true. He explained what will happen when Christ comes. When Paul mentioned those who had "fallen asleep," he referred to ___those who died___ (1 Thess. 4:13–15).

What will happen to these people at Christ's coming (1 Thess. 4:14, 16, 17)? ___Their body will return with Christ and be joined with their resurrected body___

How does Paul describe this event in 4:16–17?

- The Lord will ___descend from heaven.___
- A ___shout___
- The voice of the ___archangel___
- The ___trumpet___ of God
- The ___dead in Christ___ will rise first.
- We who are alive will be ___caught up together to meet the Lord in the air.___
- We will ___be with the Lord forever.___

Paul tells us how we can prepare for Christ's second coming. What was his advice in the following verses?

- 1 Thessalonians 4:18; 5:11: ___comfort and edify one another___
- 5:6: ___watch and be self control___

- 5:8: _put on tajit and core_
- 2 Thesslonians 2:1–3: _don't be afraid_ _faga y orkisted it frail_

CHRISTIAN LIVING

Paul gives the Thessalonians some good hints for everyday Christian living. Find them in the verses below.

- 1 Thessalonians 5:12: _respect_
- 5:13b: _be at peace_
- 5:14: _support the weak and be phtienent_
- 5:15: _dont pay evil for evil_
- 5:16: _rejoice always_
- 5:17: _pray without ceasing_
- 5:18: _give thanks in all_
- 2 Thessalonians 2:15: _stand firm_
- 3:6–10: _work and dont be idal_

THINK ABOUT IT

How would your life be different if you were actively, consistently preparing for Jesus' return?

I would constantly be worried that God will think i am not prepare

TAKE THE LEAD

WHAT'S IT ALL ABOUT?

1 & 2 Timothy are two letters…

- from _Paul_ while he was in prison at Rome the second time (1 Tim. 1:1; 2 Tim. 1:1).

- to _Timothy_ whom Paul called "_my own son in faith_" (1 Tim. 1:2).

Paul told Timothy to stay in _Ephesus_ so that he might _instruct some_ not to _teach other doctrine_ (1 Tim. 1:3). While serving in Ephesus, Timothy received two letters of encouragement and advice from Paul. Timothy probably became depressed when people did not listen to him. Sometimes people looked down on him because _young_ (1 Tim. 4:12).

Some teachers taught false doctrines that did not agree with _teaching of Christ_ (1 Tim. 6:3). Two such men who had "shipwrecked their faith" were _Hymenaeus_ and _Alexander_ (1 Tim. 1:20).

These letters told Timothy how he could serve as a good leader and teacher in the Ephesian church. How do you think these books can help us? _teach us how to be good leader_

LEADING IN WORSHIP

What instructions did Paul give Timothy about worship?

- 1 Timothy 2:1–2: Pray for _everyone_ , including _government_ officials.

- 1 Timothy 2:8: Lift up _holy hand_ in _praying_, without _angry arguments_ .

- 1 Timothy 2:9–10: Women should _dress modestly_ _____ .

- 1 Timothy 4:13: _read the word_ _thoughtful_ _____

- 1 Timothy 4:14: _use your spiritual gift_.

- 2 Timothy 2:20–21: Be a useful _vessel / instrument_ of God.

- 2 Timothy 2:22: Flee _youthful lust_ and pursue _righteousness, love, faith, peace_

LEADING OTHER LEADERS

Overseers were also called _elders_, _shepherd_ (pastors), or _bishop_. They were the leaders in each church. Find out how men became overseers in the early church by examining Acts 14:21–23 and Titus 1:5.

List fifteen things that should be characteristics of all overseers (1 Tim. 3:2–7).

1. _faithful_
2. _temperate_
3. _self controlled_
4. _respectable_
5. _hospitable_

6. _____ able to teach _____
7. _____ not given to drunkenness _____
8. _____ not violent but gentle _____
9. _____ not quarrelsome _____
10. _____ not a lover for money _____
11. _____ manage his own family well _____
12. _____ see his children obey him _____
13. _____ do it in a manner worthy of full respect _____
14. _____ not be a recent convert _____
15. _____ have a good reputation _____

Deacons (or servants) were another kind of leader in the early church.

List ten things that should be characteristics of all deacons (1 Tim. 3:8–12).

1. _____ dignified _____
2. _____ sincere or honest _____
3. _____ not given into wine _____
4. _____ not greedy _____
5. _____ hold truth not faith _____
6. _____ serious of testou _____
7. _____ blameless _____
8. _____ wives be dignified, faithful _____
9. _____ husband of one wife _____
10. _____ manage children/house well _____

LEADING THROUGH TEACHING

Define *minister*: _member of the clergy especially important church, ahead of government depart_

Paul encouraged Timothy to proclaim and teach God's Word boldly. Using the following verses, list the advice Paul gave him about teaching teachers:

1 Timothy 4:12: _be an example_

1 Timothy 4:13: _Devote yourself to reading, preaching, and teach_

1 Timothy 4:14: _use your spiritual birth gifts_

2 Timothy 1:13: _hold fast to the sound teaching others_

2 Timothy 3:16: _____

_____

THINK ABOUT IT

The letters to Timothy describe the specific qualifications and responsibilities of a pastor, but Paul is really giving good advice to anyone who wants to be a godly young person. What specific aspects of his advice should you be working more diligently to develop in your heart?

_____
_____
_____
_____

T I T U S
STAND FOR THE TRUTH

WHAT'S IT ALL ABOUT?

Titus is a letter…

- from ___Paul___, a ___servant___ _____ of God and an apostle of Jesus Christ (1:1).

- to ___Titus___, Paul's son in the sense that he shared _____ _____ (1:4).

Paul left Titus in _____ to _____ _____ and to appoint (ordain) _____ in every town (1:5).

- Where is Crete? _____ _____

Paul sailed to Crete while he was a prisoner and was on his way to Rome (Acts 27:7–13). He probably returned with Titus several years later to preach the gospel and set up churches.

- What kind of reputation did the Cretans have (1:12)?
  ___liar evil lazy___ _____

- What was Titus to do about this reputation (1:13)? ___rebuke___
  ___them sharply___ _____

Paul wrote to inform Titus of his plans to send ___Artemas___ or ___Tychicus___ to Titus so that Titus could _____ (3:12).

Paul also wrote to encourage Titus in his ministry. How did Paul encourage Titus in each of the following passages?

- 1:5: Reminded him of his job and gave direction on how to carry it out.

- 1:10–16: Warned him about ___the people who speak py___ and instructed him how to deal with them.

- 2:1, 15: Urged him to teach ___sound doctrin___ with ___authority___.

- 3:1–2: Instructed him to remind the Cretans to be subject ___to ruler___ ___and authorit___ and to live in peace with all men.

TEACH IT LIKE IT IS

A group of false teachers stirred up trouble on Crete. Paul encouraged Titus to stand his ground against them. No matter what, he was to teach the truth that he had learned from Paul.

Sometimes it is easy to doubt what we believe when all the people around us believe differently. Think how Titus must have felt. He met many intelligent people who had different ideas that sounded good. But those ideas violated the teachings of Jesus and Paul. Would you have the courage to keep on teaching what you believed? From where would such courage originate? ___God___

Who were these false teachers, and what were they teaching? Record what you learn about them in the following verses:

- 1:10: ___rebellious people___
- 1:11: ___upsetting whole house___ ___teaching things should be___
- 1:16: ___deny God know God destruction___ ___do him not obedience___
- 3:9: ___arguing for controversies___ ___and argument___

- 3:10: _divede the chunch_

To correct the false teachers and their teachings, Paul told Titus to:

- Select elders who would _hold fast to faith_
  word so that they could encourage others by sound
  teaching and _will those contradict_
  and therefore refute the opposition (1:9).

- Teach sound doctrine to:

  older men (2:2)
  older women (2:3)
  younger (2:6)

  Who was to teach the younger women?

  older women (2:3–5)

Define *doctrine*: _teaching_

- Be an example to young men by:

  good words (2:7)
  show integrity serious (2:7)
  sound speech that cannot (2:8)
  be condemned

THINK ABOUT IT

By standing for what he knew to be the truth, Titus helped the Christians in Crete
to mature. We also can help ourselves and other Christians grow up in Christ by
standing for the truth. Give an example of how you can help yourself and others
in each of the following areas:

- Teach sound doctrine. _____

  _____

- Be an example. _____

  _____

- Encourage others. _____

  _____

PHILEMON
THE RUNAWAY

WHAT'S IT ALL ABOUT?

Along with his separate letter to the Christians in the church at Colosse, Paul also sent a personal letter with Tychicus.

Philemon is a letter…

- from Paul and _Timothy_

- to Philemon—a dearly _beloved_ friend and _fellow_ _worker_ of Paul—and to _Apphia_ and _Archippus_ and the _church_ that met in their house (Phil. 1:2).

These people lived in the city of Colosse (Col. 4:17), but Paul probably met them in Ephesus. They became close friends.

ONESIMUS'S STORY

Note: The following anecdote is an imaginative picture that is consistent with the life of a first century slave but is not found in the text of Scripture.

Everyone always told Onesimus what to do. He never got to choose anything for himself. His master made him do the worst chores, such as weeding the vineyard and cleaning out the stable. Onesimus just wanted to be free.

One night he ran away from his master and hid on a ship going to Italy. He had always wanted to go to Rome, so that's the first thing he decided to do with his new freedom. But he had no food or money. When the ship's captain discovered that he was aboard, he beat him and put him to work.

At Rome, Onesimus worked hard for little pay. His stomach was never full. His back was always tired. He had no friends but beggars. He spent several months in a prison dungeon when a Jew caught him stealing.

While in prison, he heard about a man who had been brought to Rome for trial. The man was living in a rented house under house arrest. He remembered Paul, his master's friend. He remembered Paul's kindness to him at Ephesus and how Paul's religion had changed his master's life.

Onesimus found Paul and confessed to him how he had stolen from his master and fled to Rome. After Paul explained Christ's forgiveness, Onesimus became a Christian.

PAUL'S PLEA TO PHILEMON

Paul then wrote a letter to Onesimus's master, Philemon, explaining both the situation and Onesimus's change of heart.

- What did Paul ask Philemon to do (vs. 15–20)?
  to keep Onesimus back and treat each
  he was a christian.

- What did Paul hint in verses 12–14 that he would like Philemon to do?
  send Onesimus back and his help.

- What plan did Paul mention to Philemon that probably helped the master grant Paul's request (vs. 22)?
  Paul hope stay visit soon.

Paul sent Onesimus back with Tychicus, his letter-carrier (Col. 4:7–9). Tradition states that Philemon followed Paul's suggestion and sent Onesimus to him. Onesimus later became a great leader in the Colossian church.

- What does this story teach us about forgiveness? *be willing*
  to forgive others

THINK ABOUT IT

When you look at people who are less privileged or less responsible than you, what do you see? What does God see? How can you make your view of them more like God's?

_____

_____

_____

_____

_____

UNIT THIRTEEN:
THE CHURCH GROWS UP

THE BEST

THE GENERAL LETTERS

The General Letters (Hebrews through Jude) have different themes and authors. They do not tell us much history. We are not sure where all of them fit into the timeline of Acts. We know only that the writers were real people writing to real people. The writers were Jesus' spokesmen to His churches.

They are called "general letters" because they were written to a general audience. Some of them were addressed to a large group of churches, and some do not give details about the readers. We know only that their readers were people in many cities who needed advice and encouragement in the Christian life.

A MYSTERIOUS LETTER

The letter to the Hebrews is a unique letter because it does not name the sender or addressee. Other than a brief note about Timothy (13:23) and a general greeting (13:24), it reads more like an essay than a letter. It is a complicated essay that shows how Jesus fulfilled the Old Testament law.

Listen as your teacher describes this unique letter and then answer the following questions:

Why is the letter to the Hebrews unique?

it does not name the sender or
address. Essay format rather than letter

Whose name that is mentioned in the letter gives us the idea that Paul might have written it? _Timothy_

- To whom is the author writing?

  Jewish christian

- How can you better understand Hebrews?

  study ot

- What danger that the Jewish Christians faced prompted the letter?

  persecution

- How does the author of Hebrews encourage those Christians?

  Jesus is better than the old
  testament way

HE'S NOT JUST BETTER—HE'S THE BEST!

The author begins the letter by saying that in time past God spoke to their Jewish forefathers through the prophets at many times and in many ways (1:1). God used many men and many methods to communicate His Word. What method did God use to speak to men in each of the following examples?

- Genesis 28:10–22: _through a dream_
- Numbers 9:15–23: _through a cloud/fire_
- 1 Samuel 3:2–14: _spoke directly_
- 2 Kings 20:8–11: _sign_
- Ezekiel 5:1–6: _symbolic action_
- Daniel 8:1–2: _a vision_

According to Hebrews 1:2, how did God speak to men in later (more recent) days? _through his son_

This is the best way God could communicate with us—by sending His own Son to us. Jesus was the greatest Word God ever spoke (John 1:1, 14). The writer of Hebrews wanted his readers to know that Jesus brought the great message from God that the Old Testament promised. God no longer needs many prophets and many methods. He has spoken once and for all through Jesus Christ.

We have learned that Jesus is God's greatest spokesman. In Hebrews, we can see other ways in which Jesus is greater than any other man or Old Testament leader. Study the following passages and tell what makes Jesus greater:

- 1:5: _He is God's son_
- 1:8–9: _God gave him_
- 2:8–9: _God gave him authority_
- 3:1–6: _No is greater than moise_
- 4:15: _He never sinned_
- 5:8–9: _obedient by a suffering brought salvation to all who believe_
- 7:22: _Brought a better covent_
- 7:26–28: _He is a perfect high priest_
- 10:10: _By his sacrifice_

WE CAN BE THE BEST

Because we follow the best prophet, the best priest, and the best leader, we have the best religion on earth—the only true faith. How can we do our best as His followers?

- We can _pay attention to his word_ (2:1).
- We can _Fix eyes on jesus_ (3:1).
- We can _choose not to harden your heart, encourage others daily_ (3:12–13).
- We can _hold fast to our faith_ (10:22).

- We can _love one another_
  toward love and good deed (10:23).
- We can _meet together to encourage_
  one another (10:24).
- We can _praise God with our words and_
  good deeds (10:25).
- We can _____
  _____ (13:15–16).

THINK ABOUT IT

Ok, it's your turn. What is so great about Jesus? Say it in your own words. Don't just repeat what you read in your textbook.

_____
_____
_____

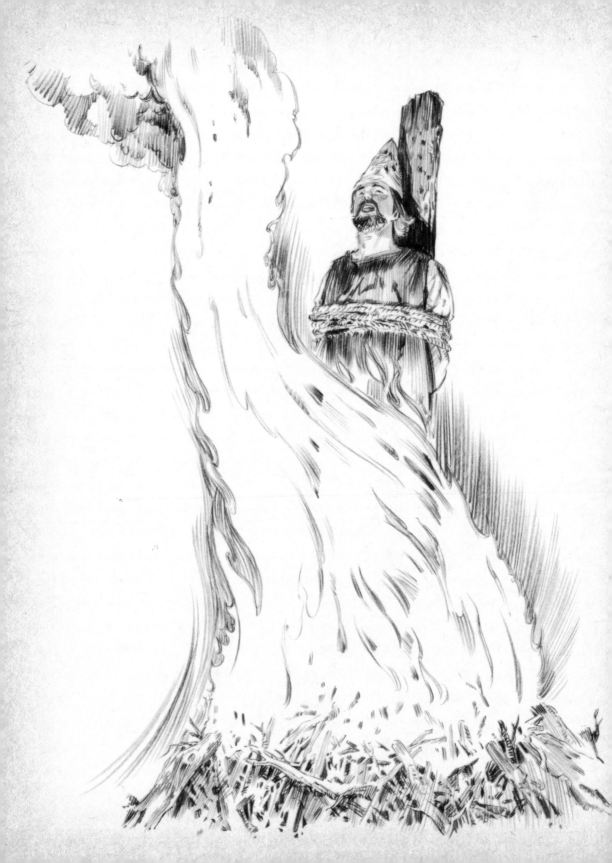

J A M E S

GET A GRIP

WHAT'S IT ALL ABOUT?

James is a letter...

- from _James_, a _servant_ of God and of the _Lord_ _Jesus Christ_ (1:1).

- to the _twelve tribes scattered abroad_ (1:1).

Which James is this? King Herod killed James, _the brother of John_ and a disciple of Jesus, in A.D. 44 (Acts 12:1–2). Another James became a leader in the _Jerusalem territory_. He was the _brother of Jesus_. Because of his respected position in the early church, it is likely that he _wrote this letter_.

Although the letter contains good advice for _Gentile_, James wrote it specifically to _Jews_. He does not name a specific geographical area but sends the letter to _Palestine_.
He wanted Jewish Christians everywhere to realize their duty to _behave like children of God_. Unbelieving Jews (and Gentiles) bullied Christian Jews. They accused them of crimes, beat them, ran them out of town, and stoned them.

Because of _persecution_, Jewish Christians began to wonder if _serving Jesus_ was really right. James wrote to encourage them in _christian living_. "No matter what happens to you," James was saying, "you can live like a Christian."

What advice does James give in the following verses?

- 1:2–3: _consider it joy when you suffer trial produce patiences_
- 1:12: _realize that god will reward you for your suffering_.
- 1:22–23: _Obey the Word_.
- 5:7: _Be patient ot Christs coming_
- What are some ways in which Christians are persecuted today?
  bully

- What advice from James that you found in the preceding verses can help you be strong when you face persecution?

  _____

  _____

GET A GRIP ON YOURSELF

James urges his fellow Christians to learn self-control. He says that we are tempted when we allow our own evil desires to take control of us (1:14). What advice does he give about self-control in the following verses?

- Control your temper by _____
  _____ (1:19–20).

- Control your _____ by _____
  _____ (1:26; 3:3–12).

- Control your desires by _____
  _____ (4:1–3).

- Control your pride by _____ (4:7), by
  _____ (4:10), and by
  _____ (4:16).

IF YOU REALLY MEAN IT, DO IT

In his letter, James tells his readers to do more than talk about their faith. "Show it!" he says. Saying that we believe something does not mean much if we never follow that belief with actions. How we live reveals what we really believe.

James gives the example of a man who looks at his face in a mirror (1:23–25). His hair is standing up. His face is dirty. His shirt is buttoned wrong. The man sees all of these things, but he walks away from the mirror without making any changes.

The Bible is like a mirror. When we look into it, we can see what we need to change about ourselves. Then we must choose whether we will make these changes. The person who listens to the Word of God but does not obey it is like the man who refuses to wash his face when he knows it is dirty.

According to 1:22, we are to be not only _____ of the Word, but also _____ of it. Otherwise we are _____ ourselves.

- According to James 2:17, what is the value of faith without action?

  _____

- How was Abraham's faith made complete (perfect) (2:21–22)?

  _____

- According to James 2:21–24, how is a person justified (made right) before God? _____

Saving faith will invariably be accompanied and demonstrated by righteous actions. A changed lifestyle is the evidence that our faith is genuine.

THINK ABOUT IT

James is about faith, but it is also about obedience. How does the way you live give evidence for your faith? _____

_____

_____

_____

I   P E T E R
WHO ARE YOU?

WHAT'S IT ALL ABOUT?

First Peter is a letter…

- from _____, an apostle of Jesus Christ (1:1).

- to the _____ (temporary residents) scattered throughout Pontus, Galatia, Cappadocia, Asia, and Bythynia (1:1).

Like James, Peter wrote to the Jewish Christians who were scattered throughout these provinces. But he also had in mind the Gentile Christians because he wrote in 2:10 that _____

_____

_____.

Peter wrote both of his letters near the end of his life, possibly from Rome. The persecution that was beginning when James wrote had become worse by the time Peter wrote his letters. According to tradition, not long after Peter wrote these letters, he was crucified upside down.

What advice did Peter give for making the best of hard times?

- 1:3–6: _____

- 2:13–14: _____

- 3:9: _____

- 3:13–15: _____

   _____

- 4:1: _____

   _____

- 4:12–16: _____
  _____

- 4:19: _____
  _____

- 5:7: _____
  _____

What will God do for those who suffer for His sake (5:10)? _____
_____
_____

HOLY LIVING

The word *holy* as used in 1 Peter 1:16, means "set apart for a specific purpose." Peter describes the purpose of the Christian life. If we follow his directions, we will be holy because we will fulfill God's purpose for our lives.

Read the following verses to discover what Peter says that we can do to be holy:

- 1:13: _____.

- 1:13: Be _____.

- 1:13: Set your hope on _____.

- 1:14: Don't conform to _____.

- 1:22: _____ one another with a pure heart _____.

- 2:1: Get rid of _____
  _____.

- 3:1–4: Wives, be _____ and be _____
  _____.

- 3:7: Husbands, be _____
  _____.

- 5:8–9: Be _____
_____.

What can you do to be more alert and ready to resist Satan?

_____

REMEMBER WHO YOU ARE

When we are pressured by temptation or face hard situations, we need to remember who we are. Peter reminds his suffering readers who they are.

Examine the following passages. In the "Who" column, tell who Peter says that we are. In the "What" column, tell what Peter says we are to do because of who we are.

Who We Are	What We Are to Do
1:2	
2:5	
2:9 • • • •	
2:11	
4:10	

THINK ABOUT IT

In which of the areas of holy living has God helped you the most? In which areas do you still *need* His help the most?

_____

_____

_____

_____

_____

2   P E T E R

IT'S THE TRUTH

(handwritten:) 3/5

WHAT'S IT ALL ABOUT?

Second Peter is a letter…

- from ___Simon Peter___, a ___servant___ and an ___apostle___ of Jesus Christ (1:1).

- to ___those who through the righteousness of our God and savior Jesus Christ have received___ (1:1). ___a faith as precious as ours___

Peter does not name precisely who his intended readers are. He does not even tell us the province(s) to which he sent it. Whoever his readers were, he writes to warn them about ___False teachers___ (2:1). List the warnings that Peter gives in the following passages:

- 2:1: False teachers will come and will ___secretly intrude destructive heresies___.

- 2:2: Many will follow their ___depraved conduct___. They will give truth a bad reputation.

- 2:3: These greedy teachers will exploit you with ___fabricated stories___.

- 2:14: They are experts in ___greed___ practices.

- 3:3: In the last days ___scoffing___ will come. They will follow their own ___evildesires___

What will happen to these false teachers?

- 2:12: _unreasoning animals_.
- 2:17: _the dark morris reselion for from forever._

Define *heresy*: _false teaching_.

HOW CAN YOU KNOW WHAT IS TRUE?

We usually trust our teachers, but sometimes certain teachers in the church teach wrong ideas. The false teachers about whom Peter wrote came into the church secretly. They deceived people by their teaching. People trusted them and did not realize how bad their teaching was.

Today, many different teachers in many different churches want to tell you what you should believe. Many of these teachers are true, but some are false. How can you tell the difference?

Marks of a true teacher:

1. His teachings match _what the bible say_.
2. He _cares_ about his students.
3. He lives _a Godly life._.

HANG IN THERE! HE'S COMING!

"Jesus is coming back!" Peter says. There will be a judgment day. The false teachers and their followers will be revealed and destroyed. Those who follow truth will be rescued from a world of lies.

He's coming! Just be patient. God is patient too. According to 2 Peter 3:9, why is God waiting before He sends His Son back to earth?

_____

_____

Peter comforts his suffering readers by reminding them that one day all suffering will end. Jesus will come suddenly when few people are expecting Him. Everything will be changed.

- What will happen to the earth and the heavens (sky and universe) after Jesus returns?

  - 3:10: _the heaven Passes away, the earth will be destroy._

  - 3:12: _the heaven will be dafter by fire_

- What promise of God can we look forward to (3:13)? _the Promise of a new heaven and earth_

Peter asks an important question in 3:11. Write the question and Peter's answers in the following spaces:

- Question (3:11): _what kind of People should we be_

- Answer (3:11): Our lives should be _holy goddy_.

- Answer (3:14): Our lives should be _peace, spotless, blameless_.

THINK ABOUT IT

Is a holy, blameless young person absolutely perfect? Is there any hope for you to be perfect? How can you make progress toward holiness? Can you do it in your own strength? _No "for all my sins, fall short to the Glory of God" romans 28.23_

1, 2, & 3 JOHN
WALKING IN THE LIGHT

WHAT'S IT ALL ABOUT?

Through these three letters, John shared wisdom gleaned from many years of experience. Notice how simple and clear the letters are. John summarized the Christian life and told how we can walk closer with God.

First John was written to a church (or churches) in Asia Minor. It was circulated among these churches and became popular reading material for worship services. John's second letter was directed to a specific church that John hoped to visit soon (vs. 12). He called this church "the elect lady." Gaius, a close friend of John, received the third letter. This man probably lived in a city not far from Ephesus because John planned to visit him soon too.

In all three letters, John has three themes. Find them in the following verses:

- 1 John 1:6; 2 John 1–2; 3 John 3–4: _truth_
- 1 John 2:3–6; 2 John 6; 3 John 11: _Obedeace_
- 1 John 3:11; 4:7; 2 John 5–6; 3 John 1: _____

THEME NO. 1—WALKING IN THE TRUTH

After reading closely the associated verses, answer the following questions:

- Where did John get his truth (1 John 1:1–3)?
  from jesus christ
- According to 1 John 1:8, how do some people deceive themselves?
  By believing the repin free

- What should these people do (1:9)? _Confessing sins_

- How can you tell if someone knows God and His truth (2:3–5)? _if they obey his word_

- According to 1 John 2:22, who is a liar? _who denies jesus christ_

- How can we know a true prophet or teacher (4:1–3)? _if they know jesus came_

- What do you think John means by "walking in truth" (2 John 4; 3 John 3–4)? _to walk with God or to walk to him_

I can walk in truth by:

- Confessing my _sin_.

- Keeping (obeying) God's _command_.

- Confessing that Jesus is the _king_.

- Confessing that _Jesus Christ_ came in the flesh.

The most important truth in the world is that Jesus, God's Son, became a man, died for our sins, rose again to give us life, and lives today.

THEME NO. 2—WALKING THE WAY JESUS WALKED

Aside from His love, one thing stands out about Jesus during His thirty-three years on earth—He always obeyed His Father. Everything He did for us was done to please His heavenly Father.

John encourages his readers to "walk as Jesus walked"—to obey God as Jesus obeyed Him.

Read the following verses to discover what a person's obedience to God proves:

- 1 John 2:3: _to know his commant_
- 1 John 2:29; 3:10: _he is righteous_ _do right to be born by him_.
- 1 John 3:24: _He dwelles in God and God lives in him_.
- 1 John 5:2–3; 2 John 6: _He loves God_

What rewards does obedience receive?

- 1 John 2:28; 3:21: _confidens before God_
- 1 John 3:21–22: _answer for prayor_
- 1 John 5:3–4: _Victory over the world_
- 2 John 8: _reward for service_

Will you walk like Jesus walked? What do you need to change in your life to walk like Him?

no, idk or everthing

THEME NO. 3—WALKING IN LOVE

According to 2 John 5, what is God's important command for us?

_____ love one anothy. _____.

List John's advice for walking in love.

- 1 John 2:9–11: _____ love your brothers/sisters
- 1 John 2:15: _____ don't love the world _____.
- 1 John 4:7: _____ love one another _____.
- 1 John 4:19–21: _____ love God and your brothers
- 1 John 5:3: _____ love God by obeying his commands

THINK ABOUT IT

What evidence do your find in your life that you are walking in the truth and that you are one of God's children?

_____

_____

_____

_____

JUDE
WATCH OUT!

WHAT'S IT ALL ABOUT?

Jude is a letter…

- from _Jude_ , a servant of Jesus Christ and a brother of _Christ_ (vs. 1).

- to those who are _____ by God the Father, and _____ in Jesus Christ, and _____ (vs. 1).

Jude is the last book in the _____ division of the New Testament.

Who is this James in verse 1 who is Jude's brother? In Galatians 1:19, he is called James, the Lord's brother. This James became a leader in the Jerusalem church. He was respected as much as the apostles. He wrote the letter of James. It is natural that Jude calls himself the brother of James in Jude 1. He would not promote himself by calling himself the brother of Jesus, although he was Jesus' half-brother.

Because he uses so many Old Testament illustrations, Jude might have written to a Jewish church. He does not name a city or province, but he has in mind particular situations about which he has heard among his readers. He does not mention any names; he simply calls them "beloved," or dear friends. Perhaps this was a general letter to many churches, some of which Jude did not know personally.

WILL THE REAL TEACHER PLEASE SPEAK UP?

Like Peter and John, Jude warned his readers about false teachers. He wrote that certain men had crept in unnoticed (Jude 4).

How did Jude describe these false teachers (Jude 4)?

_____ ungodly deny jesus chirst _____

_____

_____

Jude reminded believers that God has never tolerated such teachers who distort His Word. What examples did Jude give?

Who They Were/What They Did	What God Did
Verse 5 Isrealites did not believe	destroy them
Verse 6 Angel what keep, wa domin keep authority	keep them in dark bond with chains
Verse 7 sofom ad Gomorrah gave hin selves to perversion	set ton fire

God is patient and loving. He delays His judgment on mankind's sin, mistakes, and unbelief. He sent Jesus to pay the penalty for our sin and unbelief. But God's patience is limited.

As Christians, we must warn others about God's judgment, and we must be careful not to be deceived by false teachers.

Using the following verses, find what else Jude tells us to do to prepare for the day of judgment:

17–18: Remember that the apostles said _that all people will sroffer for not believe_.

20: Build _your sect is most holy Faith_.

20: Pray _i4the holc spirit_.

21: Keep _yourself in God's live_.

22: _Be merciful to those who doub_.

23: Save others _snatching them from thefire_.

Are you ready for the day of God's judgment? Maybe you need to change something before that day arrives. Jude has warned you. Now you have no excuse when God asks why you have not obeyed.

THINK ABOUT IT

How can you as a young person be growing in your ability to tell the difference between true and false teaching?

_____

_____

_____

_____

R E V E L A T I O N

A NEW DAY

WHAT'S IT ALL ABOUT?

Revelation 1:1 says that this last book of the Bible is the _revelation_
of _Jesus Christ_. God gave this book to show His _servants_
what must soon take place (1:1). He made it known by sending His _Angel_
to His servant, _John_ (1:1). This is the apostle John who also wrote the fourth
Gospel and three letters.

Define *revelation*: _uncover - revealing_
making something new

A MESSAGE FOR SEVEN CHURCHES

This special message from God came to John in a vision. John put it in the form
of a letter to _seven church_ (1:4).

When he wrote this letter, John was on the island of _Patmos_ because of
the word of God and
the testimonies of Jesus (1:9).

About A.D. 95, the emperor Domitian banished John from Ephesus to this island
because he preached the gospel.

Jesus appeared to John with a message for seven of His churches. On the following
table, list the seven churches to whom John wrote (1:11) and summarize what his
message (both positive and negative) to them was (See Rev. 2–3).

Church	Encouragement and Commendation	Rebuke and Warning
Ephesus	work patient endurance	need to repent
Smyrna	enduring tribulation	should not fear persecution
Pergamum	holding Fast to God name	sinful activity
Thyatira	love, Faith service	sinful activity
Sardis	somewhere still alive	bad fruit incomplete works
Philadelphia	kept God word	hold fast against assault on faith
Laodicea	nothing	materialism

JUDGMENT COMES TO EARTH

Be warned! The end comes soon.

Revelation is a book of warning. Jesus is coming to judge the world. He will reward His followers and punish His enemies. God's final message before He concluded the Bible was to warn of what is to come in the future. He wants every person to be prepared.

During the time John wrote Revelation, the Roman Empire increased its persecution of Christians. Those who read John's letter felt encouraged to know that they would one day be rescued from their suffering. Their enemies would suffer and be destroyed. Christ would triumph over all evil powers.

Chapters 4–18 issue the warning of judgment to nonbelievers and the message of comfort to Christians. Terrible things will happen, John shows. He used beasts, a dragon, angels, plagues, and many other symbols to describe the terrible days when God will judge the earth.

But John also describes the great rescue of God's people. In chapter 19, he tells of a rider on a white horse who will destroy the beast and his evil armies.

- Tell how John describes this rider (19:11–16).
  - What He was called (19:11) _Faithful and True_
  - What He did in righteousness (19:11) _Judge and make war_
  - His eyes (19:12) _blazing fire_
  - His head (19:12) _many crown_
  - His clothing (19:13) _dipped in Blood_
  - His name (19:13) _the word of God_
  - His armies (19:14) _on white horse dressed in white linen_
  - The name on His thigh (19:16) _king of kings Lord of Lords_

After reading Revelation 20:11–15, answer the following questions:

- Who do you think sits on the Great White Throne? _God_
- Who stands before the throne? _the dead_
- Which books are used to judge the dead? _the Book of Life_
- What happens to death and hell? _thrown into the lake of fire_
- What is the second death? _the lake of fire_
- What happens to a person whose name is not found in the Book of Life? _thrown in the lake of fire_
- What would you tell someone who asked you how they could ensure that his or her name is in the Book of Life? _____

A GLIMPSE OF HEAVEN

In chapter 21 John describes the new Jerusalem. No temple is needed in this city because _the lord God a Lenno bre its temple_ (21:22).

No sun or moon is needed because _CampD is liyl_ (21:23).

Find out what other things will not be in heaven by reading the following verses:

- 21:4: _death_
- 21:4: _Sorrow / mourning_
- 21:4: _crying_
- 21:4: _pain_
- 21:25; 22:5: _night_
- 21:27: _Sleepl lies shame sin_

_____

- 22:3: _curse_

The river of life flows from the throne of God down the middle of the great street of the city. What grows on each side of the river (22:2)? _tree or life_

For what are the leaves of this tree used (22:2)? _Lealing the nation_

THINK ABOUT IT

What things does the book of Revelation reveal about Jesus Christ?

_____

_____

_____

LET'S REVIEW

To review some of the material we have studied and to help yourself prepare for the final exam, complete the following exercises:

In addition to these exercises, you also should review the sixty-six books of the Bible. Half of your final exam will involve knowing these books and being able to list them in order.

	1. Malachi
	2. Judges
	3. Jonah
	4. Esther
	5. Hosea
	6. Ruth
	7. Micah
	8. Daniel
	9. Exodus
	10. Habakkuk
	11. Job
	12. 2 Samuel
	13. Zechariah
	14. Psalms
	15. Joel
	16. Nehemiah
	17. Obadiah
	18. Proverbs
	19. Genesis
	20. Amos
	21. Ecclesiastes
	22. Ezra
	23. Deuteronomy
	24. Song of Solomon
	25. Joshua
	26. Nahum

A. Tells the story of how God delivered the Israelites out of Egypt

B. Tells about how God restored the Jews to Jerusalem and the rebuilding of the temple under Zerubbabel

C. When I preached to the people of the capital of Assyria, they repented.

D. I predicted the fall of Nineveh 130 years after the revival under Jonah.

E. The story of how God brought a Moabite woman to become the wife of Boaz and the great-grandmother of David

F. A collection of wise sayings, most of which were written by Solomon

G. I spoke out against God's people holding back tithes and offerings.

H. I wrote that Edom's problem was too much pride.

I. Book about God's power in David's life

J. Tells about Israel's cycle of sin, slavery, sorrow, and salvation

K. My main question for the Lord was, "How long until you punish evil?"

L. My main message was, "Prepare to meet your God."

M. Tells about how God gave Israel victory in their conquest of the Promised Land

N. Peter quoted from my prophecy on the Day of Pentecost in Acts 2.

O. Poems or songs used as praise and worship to the Lord

P. I foretold that Christ would be born in Bethlehem.

Q. A song about love in marriage

R. God told me to marry a prostitute.

S. The story of a man who lost everything as he was tested by God

T. The story of God's providence revealed through a Jewish woman who became queen of Persia

U. Says that life is meaningless unless we fear and obey God

V. Book of how God brought all things into existence

W. I foretold more truths about Christ than any other prophet except Isaiah.

X. Contains the story of a vision given to King Nebuchadnezzar and a prophecy of how God's kingdom is greater than all others

Y. Repeats and explains the Law

Z. Tells how the walls of Jerusalem were rebuilt after the exile

	1. Matthew
	2. Ephesians
	3. Hebrews
	4. 1, 2, and 3 John
	5. Romans
	6. James
	7. Mark
	8. 1 Corinthians
	9. Philippians
	10. Philemon
	11. Acts
	12. Titus
	13. Luke
	14. Revelation
	15. 1 and 2 Thessalonians
	16. Galatians
	17. 2 Peter
	18. John
	19. Colossians
	20. Jude
	21. 2 Corinthians
	22. 1 and 2 Timothy

A. Contains Paul's instructions on being orderly in worship

B. Contains command to set your affection on things above

C. Gospel that used Jesus' miracles to prove that He was the Son of God

D. Written to emphasize the themes of truth, love, and obedience

E. Contains letter to seven churches in Asia Minor

F. Written to someone who was on an island south of Greece

G. Says "the wages of sin is death"

H. Used ninety-three quotations from the Old Testament in his Gospel

I. Shows that Jesus is better than the old covenant

J. Says Paul's goal in life was to know Christ and become like Him

K. Written to give instructions on overseers and deacons

L. Key word in his Gospel is straightway or immediately

M. Used Sodom and Gomorrah as examples of God's punishment

N. Says the focus of Paul's ministry was preaching reconciliation to Christ

O. Tells us that we need spiritual armor to fight Satan's evil forces

P. Written to clear up misunderstandings about Christ's second coming

Q. Gospel's theme is that the Son of man came to seek and save the lost

R. Says "faith without works is dead"

S. Contains Paul's offer to pay back any money that was owed

T. Says the present earth will be destroyed by fire

U. Begins with Jesus leaving His disciples and going to heaven

V. Contains the fruit of the Spirit

MULTIPLE CHOICE, OLD AND NEW TESTAMENTS

	1. What is the most important lesson we learn from Hosea's life and book?
	a. Do not divorce. b. Do not worship idols. c. God forgives us over and over again. d. God punishes us when we leave Him.
	2. What disaster happened in Judah just before Joel prophesied that he then used as an illustration of God's coming judgment?
	a. locust plague b. earthquake c. flood d. famine
	3. Jonah preached to the city of _____.
	a. Nineveh b. Tarshish c. Joppa d. Babylon
	4. Which three prophets preached to the remnant kingdom?
	a. Habakkuk, Haggai, and Malachi b. Habakkuk, Haggai, and Zechariah c. Haggai, Zephaniah, and Malachi d. Zechariah, Haggai, and Malachi
	5. The great Day of the Lord that is still future will include _____.
	a. punishment for those who disobey b. reward for God's people c. destruction of evil d. all of the above
	6. Malachi predicted that before the Messiah came, God would send _____.
	a. punishment b. Elijah c. a remnant d. all of the above

7. The capital of the northern kingdom of Israel was _____.

   a. Samaria
   b. Nineveh
   c. Babylon
   d. Jerusalem

8. The Synoptic Gospels are _____.

   a. Matthew, Mark, Luke, and John
   b. Matthew, Mark, and Luke
   c. Matthew, Mark, and John
   d. Matthew and Mark

9. Jesus grew up in the city of _____.

   a. Nazareth
   b. Bethlehem
   c. Jerusalem
   d. Capernaum

10. A short story Jesus used to teach a truth by comparison was _____.

    a. a parable
    b. an allegory
    c. a metaphor
    d. a fantasy

11. Acts is about the _____.

    a. birth of the church
    b. life of Luke
    c. Day of Pentecost
    d. history of Israel

12. Jesus told His disciples to stay in Jerusalem and wait for _____.

    a. His return
    b. the Day of Pentecost
    c. Paul
    d. the Holy Spirit

13. Philip witnessed to and baptized a man from _____.

a. Egypt
b. Ethiopia
c. Judea
d. Greece

14. God led Peter to the house of Cornelius. What did He prove to Peter there?

a. The gospel is for the Gentiles also.
b. Cornelius is a good man.
c. God wanted the gospel to spread to Samaria.
d. Peter should eat many different kinds of food.

15. Before Saul became a Christian, he _____.

a. traveled with Jesus
b. was a Roman slave
c. imprisoned and killed Christians
d. changed his name to Paul

16. Paul wrote letters to the Ephesians, Philippians, and Colossians from _____.

a. his home in Tarsus
b. prison in Rome
c. prison in Jerusalem
d. a ship sailing to Rome

17. The theme of the letter to the Philippians is _____.

a. humility
b. joy
c. love
d. prayer

18. The theme of 1 & 2 Timothy is _____.

a. humility
b. unity
c. leadership
d. love

19. The General Letters are called "general" because they _____.

a. do not tell who wrote them
b. do not tell to whom they are written
c. cover many general topics
d. were sent to a wide, general audience

20. We can better understand the letter to the Hebrews by _____.

a. knowing for sure who wrote it
b. studying the Old Testament
c. studying the book of Acts
d. talking to Jews in our community

21. The letter of James was most probably written by _____.

a. James, the brother of John
b. James, the brother of Jesus
c. James, the bishop of Rome
d. someone who used James' name so people would read what he had written

22. Peter wrote his first letter to _____.

a. Christians scattered over Asia Minor
b. Christians in Rome
c. Christian Jews
d. Christians in Jerusalem

23. John wrote Revelation while in _____.

a. Ephesus
b. prison at Rome
c. exile on the island of Patmos
d. Jerusalem

24. Jude wrote to warn his readers about _____.

a. false letters
b. false teachers
c. Satan's angels
d. all of the above

25. The second death in Revelation 20 is _____.

a. the lake of fire
b. death in sin
c. physical death
d. none of the above